ROMAN POMPEII

Space and society

Ray Laurence

London and New York

First published 1994
by Routledge
11 New Fetter Lane, London EC4P 4EE

Simultaneously published in the USA and Canada
by Routledge
29 West 35th Street, New York, NY 10001

First published in paperback 1996

Typeset in Garamond by
Florencetype Ltd, Kewstoke, Avon
Printed and bound in Great Britain by
Biddles Ltd, Guildford and King's Lynn

British Library Cataloguing in Publication Data
A catalogue record for this book is available from the British Library

Library of Congress Cataloguing in Publication Data
Laurence, Ray.
Roman Pompeii: space and society/Ray Laurence.
p.   cm.
Includes bibliographical references and index.
1. Pompeii (Extinct city)   2. City planning – Italy –
Pompeii (Extinct city)   I. Title.
DG70.P7L38   1994
937'.7–dc20   93–42553

ISBN 0–415–09502–6 (hbk)
ISBN 0–415–14103–6 (pbk)

CONTENTS

FIGURES, MAPS AND PLATES

FIGURES

MAPS

PLATES

PREFACE

This book is about Pompeii – a city much studied by others. However, the social meaning of Pompeii has seldom been addressed. Pompeii is an archaeological artefact of immense complexity: after all, it was a city. At times it may appear that I explain aspects of this artefact in historical terms, at others in a more archaeological framework. As a result this book might be seen by some (e.g. Klejn 1993) as an academic heresy. However, the past should be approached from both perspectives. After all, both subjects seek to explain the same object – the past. The division between these two disciplines is hard to conceptualise. Archaeology confronts history, and history confronts archaeology. By archaeology, I do not mean the narrow perspectives of classical archaeology. The influence of the debates in theoretical archaeology, conducted principally by prehistorians, can be identified in what follows. Too often, ancient historians and classical archaeologists have isolated themselves from the main debates in archaeology and history. Therefore, I have sought to interpret the Pompeian evidence in the light of developments in archaeology and history. I have also drawn upon the methods and preoccupations of architects, geographers and social scientists. The object has been to explain the ancient city of Pompeii in its social and spatial context; and above all to interpret the evidence. The book contains both my own research and a synthesis of the work of others. The latter is included to make Pompeii more accessible to a wider audience. It will be noted that I have concentrated upon public space and social interaction, at the expense of the private or domestic context. There is a reason for this. Domesticity in Pompeii is being approached from a number of new angles, and much of this work has yet to be published. In fact, in the near future, we may look forward to a revolution in the way the Pompeian house is studied. Until this work is published, it will not be possible to account for domestic space in Pompeii adequately. Thus, I leave it to one side and examine primarily public space and the social interaction that took place within it.

The reader should be aware of the Pompeian reference system. The archaeological site was divided into nine regions by Fiorelli in the nineteenth century. These are numbered 1–9. In each region, the *insulae* (blocks) were numbered and each doorway in an *insula* was given a number. Therefore, each location of, say, a house is referred to thus: 9.1.2. In this case, the first number refers to the region, the second number refers to the *insula* block and, finally, the third number refers to the entrance to the building. This allows for easy location of buildings on the site and also on maps of Pompeii.

All references in the text follow the Harvard system, or are standard classical references to ancient texts. References to modern works have been kept under control and tend to refer to the most accessible material available.

Newcastle
August 1993

ACKNOWLEDGEMENTS

Thanks are due to many people who have helped me in my research into Roman urbanism. In Newcastle, Jeremy Paterson (the supervisor of my Ph.D.) has consistently offered help and advice. My Ph.D. examiners, Nicholas Purcell and Tony Spawforth, deserve the warmest thanks for their sound and critical comment. Nicholas Purcell and Andrew Wallace-Hadrill pointed me in the direction of a book about Pompeii, rather than the wider subject of urbanism in Roman Italy: a proposal which received further encouragement from Richard Stoneman. In Pompeii, Baldassare Conticello granted me permission to visit the whole site and Mattia Buondonno made my visit considerably easier. The British School at Rome assisted me financially with two short grants from the Hugh Last fund and a scholarship in 1990–1. None of this would have been possible without their financial support or the library facilities of the school run so humanely by Valerie Scott and her staff. There are many others who deserve thanks. Nearly all the material in the book was presented at numerous seminars and conferences in Leicester, London, Rome, Reading and Newcastle. Rhiannon Evans commented on the final draft. Map 3.3 is reprinted by permission of the Peters Fraser & Dunlop Group Ltd. The plan of the house of the Vettii, Figure 7.1, is taken from Wallace-Hadrill (1988), fig. 10, with permission from the British School at Rome. I would like to thank two reviewers, Alison Davies and Michele George, for letting me have their critical comments which I have followed in correcting the text for the paperback edition. Further, I would like to thank Alison Davies for supplying me with her unpublished map of locations of inscriptions in the forum, which I used to correct Figure 2.3. My greatest debt is due to Jeremy Paterson, who has found time to discuss, argue, enthuse and offer constructive advice over a number of years. Any errors that remain are my own.

INTRODUCTION

Pompeii is one of the most famous archaeological sites in Europe. The thousands of people who visit the remains of this Roman city each day of the year are brought into close proximity to a past which has been preserved by the eruption of Vesuvius in AD 79. As visitors walk down the streets, the scale and nature of the remains make it easy for them to create their own idea of an urban society in the first century AD. This experience of the Roman city draws upon the physical reality of the past as it has been preserved: the forum, the houses, the brothels, the theatres, the amphitheatre and, of course, the plaster casts of the dead (Etienne 1992 and Connolly 1979 provide excellent introductions to the site for those who have not visited Pompeii). Frequently, these reconstructions are distinctly idealised. Some of these utopias find their way into art and literature (Leppmann 1968). Other images and experiences of Pompeii are absorbed into modern architecture and town planning (Unwin 1909), and are indirectly experienced by those living in the modern twentieth-century cities of Western Europe. Pompeii exists not only in the past but also in the present. The visitors to this ancient city find it is so like their own urban experience in the modern world that they interpret what they see in the light of their knowledge of the modern city. Everything appears to be easily understood and laid out by the heritage industry.

In contrast, Pompeii reveals a very different reality to the 'professional' archaeologist or historian. Although Pompeii has undergone more than two hundred years of excavation and conservation, this has had a relatively small impact upon the disciplines of archaeology and ancient history. The reasons for this have been summed up by Wallace-Hadrill:

> It [Pompeii] is at once the most studied and the least understood of sites. Universally familiar, its excavation and scholarship prove a nightmare of omissions and disasters. Each generation discovers with horror the extent to which information has been ignored, neglected, destroyed and left unreported and unpublished.
>
> (Wallace-Hadrill 1990: 150)

1

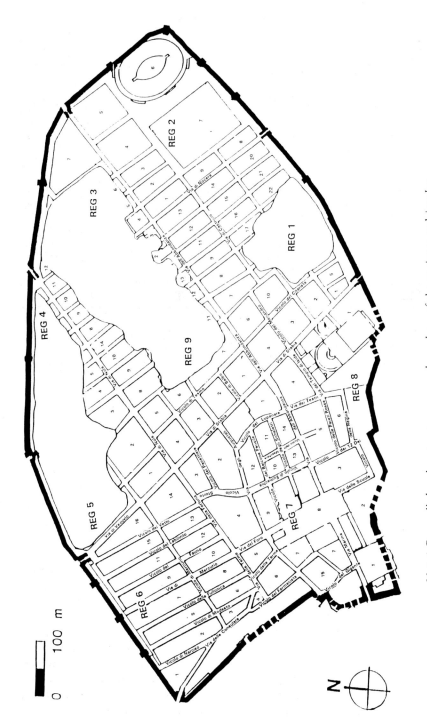

Map 1 Pompeii showing street names, and numbers of the *regiones* and *insulae*

Plate 1 The fabric of Pompeii (Vicolo del Balcone Pensile)

The information that is the most accessible for study, at Pompeii, is the physical fabric of the ancient city: the architecture and wall painting. This material is most readily available, whilst it remains conserved. In contrast, the artefacts found alongside the physical fabric of the city have in many cases been lost or dispersed, and can only be rediscovered via the reports of the excavators of the site. This situation has caused much scholarship in the twentieth century to concentrate upon the art and architecture at the expense of a broader cultural investigation of Pompeian society. Even for those scholars interested in art and architecture, Pompeii presents problems. In those areas away from the most-visited parts of the site, vegetation often obscures the object of study (Descœudres and Sear 1987: 13). This can cause areas of the site to be neglected and not examined. The general deterioration of the archaeological remains should not be under-estimated (Adam 1980; Ioppolo 1992). The costs of preservation are enormous upon such a large site. The excavated area, forty-four hectares of the total sixty-six-hectare site, requires funding to the tune of 1,500 billion lire, but the present level of funding only comes to some seventy billion lire (letter from Conticello in the *Guardian*, 20 January 1993).

In the face of the deterioration of the physical fabric a number of initiatives have been taken to record the site. From 1975, an international project, Häuser in Pompeji, has been running to record individual houses with exceptional wall decoration (Strocka 1984, 1991; Michel 1990; Ehrhardt 1988; Seiler 1992; Descœudres and Sear 1987; Eschebach 1982; Peters 1993). Also, in the late 1980s, a computer data-base was set up to record the site (Conticello 1990: this supersedes earlier photographic records, e.g. Vlad Borelli *et al.* 1983). This work is still at an early stage. Alongside the work on the computer data-base, an attempt is being made to re-examine and publish some of the lesser-known buildings from Pompeii. In doing so, the authors use the original excavation reports to establish in what state the structure was found, rather than what is preserved today. Also, they have chosen remarkable buildings: the Casa del Marinaio, with a store building on its lower level, and the Sarno bath complex, which may resemble the architecture of the *insulae* at Ostia (Franklin 1990; Ostrow 1990). Such work can only partially compensate for the loss of evidence in the past.

There has also been a re-evaluation of our ways of interpreting Pompeian evidence. The method of dating the fabric of Pompeii, which is based upon a typology of masonry fabric and wall painting (the four styles) has been seriously questioned (Dwyer 1991; Allison 1992a; 1992b; Wallace-Hadrill 1990; Laidlaw 1985. Contra: Strocka 1991). The critics of this traditional schema have made a strong argument for a more contextual approach to the *atrium* house. Such an approach would examine the finds, the decoration and the architecture together. Only then could a dating sequence be constructed. However, without further excavation below the AD 79 destruction level, such an ambition will continue to remain unfulfilled (recent excavations below the destruction level: Arthur 1986; Nappo 1988; Bonghi Jovino 1984. See also recent excavation reports in *Rivista di Studi Pompeiane*). One dating point that continues to have a role is the earthquake of AD 62. This earthquake, according to Seneca (*N.Q.*6), caused considerable damage to the physical fabric of the city (Andreau 1973; Guidoboni 1989: 139–67 lists epigraphic evidence). The extent of the damage to the city is difficult to evaluate, not least because the eruption of Vesuvius in AD 79 was also accompanied by an earthquake (Plin.,*Ep.* 6.16, 6.20). The supposition of 'extensive' earthquake damage in AD 62 has been used to account for a variety of social change in Pompeii (e.g. Nappo 1988; Castiglione *et al.* 1989; Carocci *et al.* 1990). At its most extreme, this form of explanation has been used to attribute a rise of an urban bourgeoisie, which replaced the traditional elite whose fortunes were based upon landed wealth. Mouritsen has exposed the simplistic nature of this argument. He argues that rather than seeing a municipal elite that was closed off to other groups, we should view Pompeian society as fluid with new members entering the *ordo* of decurions frequently throughout Pompeii's history (Mouritsen forthcoming; 1988).

The economic basis for the rise of the bourgeoisie had already been questioned by Andreau (1973). The earthquake of AD 62 would have had a dramatic effect upon urban life, as we shall see in Chapter 2, but there is always a danger that a dated event in a literary source can dominate and eradicate other forms of explanation of social change.

The re-examination of the epigraphic evidence in Pompeii has led to a total rejection of the methods of Della Corte (1965). Mouritsen (1988: 13–27) argues forcefully that the electoral *dipinti* on the façades of houses were not, in most cases, related to the owners or occupiers of those houses; so we can no longer attribute ownership of a house upon the basis of the graffiti on the façade. Equally, the social status of the occupiers of the houses cannot be established solely upon stylistic grounds. Wallace-Hadrill (1990) has proposed through a sample of *insulae* in *Regiones* 1 and 6 that there was a unified material culture that does not highlight discrepancies between wealth and poverty.[1] Wallace-Hadrill's re-evaluation (1991) of the population of sampled houses and the city as a whole results in similar feelings of frustration. We cannot securely attribute exact numbers of inhabitants to many of the houses in the city (contra Strocka 1991).[2] Many of our problems of interpretation are aggravated by the incomplete recording and publication of the finds from Pompeii (Wallace-Hadrill 1990: 187–9; Carandini 1977). A further problem is encountered when the finds are examined. In many ways, the deposition of this material is more complicated than previously thought. Allison has found evidence of hoarding, looting and clearance of valuables from houses prior to and shortly after the eruption of AD 79 (Allison 1992a, 1992b). Until we fully understand this depositional phase, little can be extrapolated from the evidence of the finds from individual houses in isolation. For example, what are the implications of the finds from *Insula* 1.8? A large number of coins, totalling six hundred sesterces, were found at a bar 1.8.8–9 (Castiglione *et al.* 1989; compare Crawford 1970: 42 and 1969 no. 245); in contrast relatively few coins were found elsewhere in the *insula* (see Figure 1). Does the sum found at the bar represent a day's takings, or the total capital of the owner of the bar? Did the occupiers of the rest of the *insula* need such sums of monetary wealth, or had these inhabitants left with their money? The latter seems likely, because if we compare the distribution of coin finds to finds of *amphorae* in the *insula*, we find that there is a more even distribution of stored or consumed wealth (*amphorae*) than of movable wealth (coinage) (see Figure 1). The question of how this may reflect social gradations within the *insula* remains uncertain. However, it should be recognised that the coin find at 1.8.8–9 included a significant number of coins from a much earlier period: see Figure 2. Still, we are not sure if these are in circulation or not. What is clear is that Pompeian material culture is cumulative. Dated artefacts such as coins reveal a longevity that should not be dismissed. A similar situation is revealed by dated *amphorae* in *CIL* 4 (2551–9, 5511–28, 9313–17, 10261): see Figure 3. Twenty-one per cent of all dated *amphorae* were more than thirty years old when Vesuvius erupted. Thus, any artefact assemblage found in a house at Pompeii reflects the accumulated wealth of the inhabitants over more than a single generation. Any interpretation of the finds remains limited until more material is published and evaluated. Such evaluation should be conscious of the wider issues of archaeological deposition. For the 'professional' archaeologist, unlike the guided visitor, Pompeii presents a complex problem that requires solution, but such problem solving is bedevilled by an unsatisfactory body of data, at least for the immediate future. However, such reasoning should not excuse us from an evaluation of the evidence that is available. It is a fallacy that incomplete data cannot be used in the explanation of archaeological phenomena. In the case of Pompeii, this has resulted in an almost complete neglect of the site by archaeologists working upon methodological and theoretical issues (but note Raper 1977). The scope for such work is immense (Dyson 1993). In fact, academic archaeology's relative neglect of Pompeii, the largest urban site in Europe, cannot be excused. In the future, we can look forward to a more rigorous discussion of our methods of interpretation, and theoretical approaches to this unique body of evidence.

The 'professional' historians have also, in the past, neglected Pompeii as a source of evidence and as an object of study. Pompeii was seen as a place for the study of art and architectural history and also of the mechanics of elections under the empire (Wallace-Hadrill 1988: 48). However, more recently, there has been a reassessment of what Pompeii represents and how

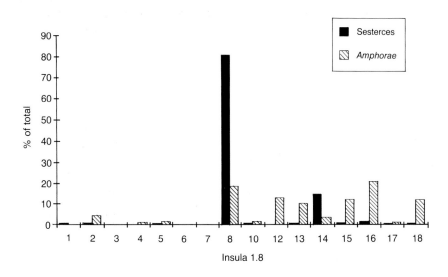

Figure 1 Percentage of total finds from *Insula* 1.8 found at each address

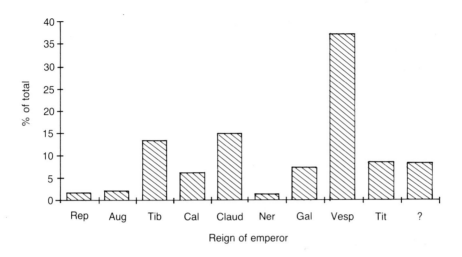

Figure 2 Coins found at 1.8.8/9

we should use such evidence. There was seen to be a real need to relate literary texts, giving details about social life, to the archaeological evidence. The aim was not to explain the evidence in literary texts but, rather, to examine the underlying social use and meaning of the archaeological data (Wallace-Hadrill 1988: 46). This reassessment of the evidence has concentrated upon the *atrium* house, which is seen to be closely related to the social standing of its inhabitant (Wallace-Hadrill 1990). In conducting his study of Pompeian housing, Wallace-Hadrill (1990: 190–2) has examined a sample

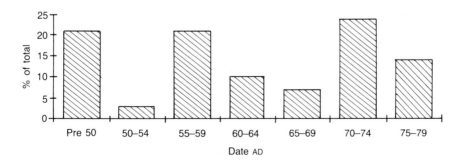

Figure 3 Amphorae with dated *tituli* in *CIL* 4

7

of 122 houses and differentiates them according to size, function, architecture and decoration. Rather than being a conclusive study of social status and housing, his quantified results present a picture of a diffusion of luxury products from the elite throughout the city of Pompeii. The real value of such work comes out in the application of literary evidence to the explanation of the functions and activities of Roman social life (Dwyer 1991 and, in particular, Wallace-Hadrill 1988). The *atrium* house was well adapted to the rituals of visiting at the *salutatio* and at dinner. The house was equally well arranged for household rituals of a religious nature (summarised by Clarke 1991: 1–29). In this context, the decoration and architecture of the *atrium* house embodied the occupier's social power (Wallace-Hadrill 1991: 226). Moreover, the implications of the Pompeian evidence for the study of a variety of topics in Roman history, for example the Roman family, cannot be underestimated. Pompeii provides a context that can place a control upon the interpretation of our disparate literary sources. For example, housing in Pompeii provides a variety of contexts in which the Roman family existed (Wallace-Hadrill 1991: 225). This underlies the complex relationship between the archaeological evidence from Pompeii and the literary source material. The relationship is reflexive. Literary sources can inform us about the 'social rhythms' that underlie the material culture (Wallace-Hadrill 1988: 48).

Equally, archaeological data from Pompeii can also reveal that missing context that is assumed by our literary sources. In effect, one informs the other. The relationship is not a simple one and needs to be handled with care. Simplistic applications of literary evidence to archaeological data, so common in the past, must be avoided (Allison 1992a, 1992b). The temptation to reject the literary source material, because it may be unrepresentative, biased, incomplete and from a different context, in favour of a 'purer' archaeological explanation should also be resisted. If we reject the literary sources, we are discarding a body of evidence that is as much a cultural product of Roman society as the archaeological evidence itself. Not to use such evidence to inform our own interpretation of the evidence from Pompeii is the equivalent of ignoring the implications of archaeological evidence for the study of Roman socioeconomic history (Jongman 1988 expects too much of the archaeological evidence). Both archaeological and literary sources have their relevance for the study of Pompeii, but these sources need to be deployed with care in our interpretation and writing about Pompeii's past existence. Ideally, the historical/archaeological interpretation should satisfy both disciplines. In what follows, both archaeological and literary sources are used to elucidate the nature of the urban experience of the inhabitants of Pompeii.

In the wider context of the study of Roman history, Pompeii has played its part in the definition of the nature of the Roman economy. Not surprisingly, Pompeian evidence was used to reinforce Rostovtzeff's conception of the Roman economy, as closely similar to that of Western Europe and North America in the early twentieth century (Rostovtzeff 1957: 61–73). Rostovtzeff's analysis was by simple analogy between the ancient and modern objects, such as towns or coins (Greene 1986: 14). Stress was placed upon traded goods and the rise of a bourgeoisie. The city was seen to have been a producer of goods similar to the modern cities of the early twentieth century (Rostovtzeff 1957: xii–xiv). It was argued, by Moeller, that one of the major products of Pompeii was textiles, which was organised by a guild structure, similar to those associated with medieval Europe (Moeller 1976). Such a simplistic analysis has been effectively destroyed by Jongman's (1988) work on the Pompeian economy. He exposes the paucity of methodology that was associated with the 'modernising' assumptions of Moeller and others (Jongman 1988: 155–86). His work attempted to substantiate the Finley model of the 'consumer city'. This model had been eloquently set out by Finley (1973) in *The Ancient Economy* and was based upon Weber's ideal types of the city (Weber 1958). Finley (1973) had suggested that the ancient economy was embedded in the social structure and the value system of Roman society. He pointed to a passage of Cicero (*Off.* 1.150–1) that suggested that production and trade were unwisely indulged in. Finley concluded that given these social values trade was socially taboo. This outlook derived from literary evidence was combined with Weber's model of the 'consumer city'. The 'consumer city', in contrast to the 'producer city', did not produce manufactured goods for export to external markets. Instead, in the 'consumer city', the agricultural surplus of the city's rural hinterland was consumed by the elite in the city. Where manufacturing was undertaken, it was to service the elite with luxury products for conspicuous consumption in the city (Finley 1973: 123–49; Weber 1958: 65–90). This model of the city does not deny that the ancients used coins, traded, manufactured goods, or lived in towns, but what they did not do was to manufacture goods explicitly for an economic trade with external markets (for excellent discussion of Finley's work see Jongman 1988: 28–54 and Greene 1986: 14–16). Although the 'consumer city' model is very neat and concise, and has become the new orthodox view of how we should view the city and the economy of the Roman Empire, it was not without its critics, who continued to adhere to the modernising concepts derived from Rostovtzeff and others (e.g. D'Arms 1981). To settle this debate once and for all, Jongman applied the model of the 'consumer city' to the extant remains of Pompeii. The model seems to fit the Pompeian evidence, but some evidence is explained away by Jongman (1988: 97–110).[3] Furthermore, Jongman only analyses the archaeological evidence to discredit the theories of others, most notably Moeller, and does not use this source of information to reinforce or falsify his own arguments (e.g. when dealing with *amphorae*, Jongman 1988: 124–30). In many ways, his analysis of

Plate 2 Street junction with fountain: note the older well head behind the fountain

Pompeii could have referred to almost any theoretical ancient city. Primarily, he refined the work of Finley and applied it to a geographical location, rather than to an archaeological situation. Such work could have been conducted upon any city in Campania which has a known geographical location.[4] However, given these criticisms of Jongman's application of the model, we have to recognise that the 'consumer city' is by far the best available model that actually defines an ancient city in economic terms (for alternatives see Carandini 1988: 327–38; Engels 1990, to be read with the review by Saller 1991).

In the following chapters, the Pompeian evidence is examined to highlight the role of the city. This analysis is not confined to proving or disproving the validity of the 'consumer city' model. Certainly, the analysis may highlight the appropriateness or otherwise of the model, but this is not the primary purpose of the book. Underlying the analysis given in the following chapters is the reflexive relationship between urban space and the activities that were conducted by the inhabitants in that space. It has frequently been observed that all behaviour has a spatial aspect to it. For example, the tombs of the dead were located outside the city walls. Should we see individual

Pompeians choosing to locate the dead outside the city or did the individual Pompeian have no choice but to place the tomb of a relative there because the dead were spatially located outside the city? In effect, people are born into a spatial world, in which the individual has only a limited choice about the location of activities. However, individuals can fundamentally alter the fabric of urban space. This view of the individual and urban space at times seems to approach a tautology, but this only further underlines the reflexive relationship between space and society. The two entities, space and society, cannot be neatly separated. One is constantly acting upon the other and, simultaneously, the opposite is occurring. Throughout the book, urban activities are analysed within their spatial context. Chapter 1 seriously questions the assertion, within Pompeian studies, that the city was planned. It will be argued that the layout of streets was produced by factors that should not be associated, primarily, with town planning. Chapter 2 examines how the identity of the city was altered from the colonial foundation to the city's destruction in AD 79. The focus is upon the development of civic architecture that reflected the changing identity of Pompeii in this period. In Chapter 3, the level of analysis moves on to a study of local identity and territory within the city. The concepts of neighbours and neighbourhood are fundamental to this study, which utilises the evidence for the distribution of local shrines and the public water supply at a local level. Chapter 4 addresses the location of productive workshops and the nature of production in the city. In particular, the question of whether workshops were concentrated in defined areas is considered. In Chapter 5, deviant behaviour that might have outraged some inhabitants is examined to highlight, for example, whether certain areas of the city were more tolerant of the presence of prostitutes. In Chapter 6, the emphasis shifts to the physical fabric of the city. Through analysis of the use of street frontages, levels of activity are attributed to streets within the city. This highlights streets with high and low levels of human activity in them. In Chapter 7, the spatial arrangement of the buildings adjoining the streets is analysed to establish how the spatial pattern of activity, discussed in Chapter 6, was produced. Chapter 8 examines the variation in the use of space through the day. This establishes a temporal framework, a social product, which placed constraints upon the use of urban space. Finally, in Chapter 9, the themes of the book are drawn together to unify the competing views of Pompeii set out in the individual chapters. This final chapter also places Pompeii in the wider context of the study of the Roman city. The implications of the reflexive relationship of urban space and urban society, so apparent in Pompeii, are used to establish a more coherent and all-embracing view of the Roman city.

1

ANCIENT AND MODERN TOWN PLANNING

Pompeii was a planned city, like many other Roman cities – or so it is generally asserted by scholars. However, what is meant by 'planned' in this context? Roman colonies founded on green-field sites display Roman planning at its most elaborate. The streets and public space were laid out along geometric lines, which suggests an ordered arrangement. But this has little in common with the modern conception of town planning, which is a complex process for the organisation of modern cities. This modern town planning, unlike Roman 'planning', not only lays out a street pattern, but also organises the use of space and takes account of topography, local transport needs, social concerns, economic parameters, conservation and environmental issues, to name but a few. In contrast, what is known as 'ancient town planning' only addressed the problem of how the city should be laid out. It was Haverfield, the Oxford historian, who originally asserted the notion of the planned Roman city in 1913. His interpretation of ancient towns as planned has never been questioned and has been reproduced recently by Owens (1991). However, in our assessment of urban space in Pompeii, we need to examine how useful the term 'town planning' is for the study of the ancient city. Therefore, in this chapter, the nature of modern and ancient town planning will be evaluated.

Haverfield's book *Ancient Town Planning*, published in 1913, was based on two lectures given in 1910: the Creighton lecture to the University of London and a paper given at the London Conference on Town Planning. The book was not only a study of ancient town planning but also had a strong political message for the twentieth-century reader. As Haverfield stated in the preface:

> The original lecture was written as a scholar's contribution to a modern movement. It looked on town planning as one of the new methods of social reform, which stand in somewhat sharp contrast with the usual aims of political parties and parliaments.
>
> (Haverfield 1913: 2)

In many ways, Haverfield's interpretation was fundamentally influenced by the modern town-planning movement. Therefore to understand his interpretation of town planning, it is necessary to assess the influences upon his original interpretation of Roman city plans.

In the nineteenth century, Britain's cities had undergone a period of rapid growth in both population and area. This growth had been unregulated and, in consequence, the environmental impact had been catastrophic. It was in the period 1900–14 that there was a general realisation of the effects of rapid urbanisation. The statistical surveys of Charles Booth and others had demonstrated that the problem was more widespread than previously thought. This new perception of the urban problem gave rise to a series of intellectual and political ideas that crossed party lines and permeated all levels of society. Britain's failure in the Boer War was blamed upon the poor health of potential recruits. In 1902, for example, 50 per cent of all recruits from Manchester were rejected because of their poor physique. The report of the Interdepartmental Committee on Physical Deterioration, in 1904, associated the poor health of army recruits with overcrowding, atmospheric pollution and other effects of urban living (Ashworth 1965: 167–90; Cherry 1988: 49–73). Therefore, the problems of the cities of Britain were seen, for the first time, to concern the nation. This feeling was summed up by Horsfall in 1908:

> Unless we at once begin at least to protect the health of our people by making the towns in which most of them now live, more wholesome for body and mind, we may as well hand over our trade, our colonies, our whole influence in the world, to Germany without undergoing all the trouble of a struggle in which we condemn ourselves beforehand to certain failure.
>
> (From T.C. Horsfall, *The Relation of Town Planning to the National Life* (1908), quoted by Ashworth 1965: 169)

The health of the nation was a cause célèbre of the eugenics movement. Its main concern was the racial degeneration of the British people, in particular, in relation to the rising number of insane (e.g. 1872, 2.2 per 1,000 insane, 1909, 3.2 per 1,000 insane) and also to the decline of the birth rate in the cities (Searle 1976). At the same time, there was a strong campaign for national efficiency, which stressed, amongst other things, the need for industry to be located close to railway yards, and that residential areas should be located away from these areas (Searle 1971). Thus, in effect, this campaign was an early assertion of the need for zoning in the city.

An alternative to these authoritarian campaigns was put forward by the Garden City Association. From 1899, Ebenezer Howard had been asserting that the solution to Britain's urban problems was to create an attractive alternative to urban life, which could be economically sustained. His solution was the Garden City, an ideal form, which he presented in the terminology acceptable to the establishment and, above all, in practical terms. The foundation of Letchworth (1903) firmly demonstrated this. Moreover, the Garden City Association was an important pressure group, which organised conferences on town planning in 1907 and 1908 and also held lectures throughout the country. The appeal of Garden Cities was not to any one group, but crossed political, religious, social and class lines (Hardy 1991).

The out-pouring of articles and books in this period advocating town planning is immense. Articles appeared in the *Builder*, the *Sociological Review*, the *Architectural Review* and others, such as the *Race-Builder*. Books on town planning began to appear from 1906 with Patrick Geddes' *City Development*, to be followed by Raymond Unwin's *Town Planning in Practice* in 1909, which sold widely. It was with such pressure that the first Town Planning Act was passed in 1909, which acknowledged that city development could no longer be subject to market forces alone.

It should be noted that the advocates of town planning looked to the past for examples to justify their position. In particular, it was the Roman Empire that attracted them. The Roman Empire was an urban culture. It was perceived as a strong empire geared up for conquest. The level of urban amenity and architecture impressed itself upon the early twentieth-century mind. The organised street grid and aesthetic appearance of the ancient city were also important in justifying the civilised nature of a planned urban environment (see, e.g., Unwin 1909: 27–52). Therefore, it should come as no surprise that at the RIBA's 1910 Town Planning Conference there was a morning devoted to 'Cities of the past', and that three of the four papers were upon the ancient world.

The 1910 Town Planning Conference marked a high point for town planning in Britain. Never before or since has town planning been granted such high esteem. There were 52 papers, 1,200 delegates, and an exhibition at the Royal Academy.[1] In the session 'Cities of the past', Gardner gave an informative account of the Greek city, Haverfield highlighted town planning in the Roman world, Ashby delivered a paper on Rome and Brinckmann accounted for the ideal of town planning from the Renaissance to the present. Haverfield's paper linked modern and ancient planning, with a strong case for a system of planning in the modern world based upon a grid of streets. One of the problems for those, such as Haverfield, who see planning throughout the Roman world is the city of Rome itself. The capital of the Roman Empire displays none of the qualities of planning that had been highlighted by Gardner and Haverfield. This had been recognised by Livy (5.55), who provided an inadequate explanation for the lack of planning in the capital. This lack of planning in Rome was highlighted by Ashby, the Director of the British School at Rome, in his paper. He explained the form of ancient Rome with reference to the physical topography of the site and structural features, in particular the Servian wall. Moreover, he railed against the current tendency of planning in Rome based upon the grid without any respect to extant topography. Significantly, the full force of the town-planning lobby, present at the conference, brushed aside Ashby's discussion of ancient Rome and his objections to modern planning founded upon geometric ideals. In the discussion after the papers, Lanciani highlighted the replanning of Ostia in a fashion similar to an American city. The link between the Roman past and the present was well received by the delegates.[2] The conference itself and, in particular, the session on 'City development and extension' seem to have made an impression on Haverfield and caused him to examine the work of Stübben and Unwin in greater detail (Haverfield 1913: 4 note 1).

Following the 1910 conference, Haverfield revised his paper for publication in book form. The conference paper and *Ancient Town Planning* reveal his feelings about town planning. He insisted that modern and ancient life were not different (Haverfield 1910: 123). He suggested that there should be a system of town planning similar to the Roman grid formation: 'The square and the straight line are indeed the simplest marks which divide civilised man from the barbarian' (Haverfield 1910: 124). He had little time for the recent German planning based upon the curve: 'It has remained for the Teutonic spirit in these last days to connect civilisation with the curve' (Haverfield 1910: 124). For Haverfield, town planning, whether modern or ancient, was: 'the art of laying out towns with due care for the health and comfort of the inhabitants, for industrial and commercial efficiency, and for reasonable beauty' (Haverfield 1913: 11). Here we see the influence of the campaign for national efficiency, alongside Geddes' sociological approach to city planning (on Geddes see Boardman 1978 and Meller 1990). Also, under the influence of Geddes, he asserted that the ancient city under the empire served a region, with its amenities of the amphitheatre and theatre. To back this up, he cited the example of Nucerians attending the amphitheatre at Pompeii in AD 59 (Tac., *Ann*.14.17). It is specifically with reference to Pompeii that we see the permeation of modern ideas about twentieth-century planning into Haverfield's analysis of the ancient city (Haverfield 1913: 63–8). He explicitly rejected Mau's conclusion that the excavated street pattern of Pompeii was laid out in a single phase. Instead, he concluded, from an examination of the plan of the site, that the town had expanded in a number of stages from a smaller nucleated settlement, which was located to the west of the city. This he termed the *Altstädt*, which he associated with the irregular streets close to the forum (a view followed by many today, e.g. Ling 1991). From its original foundation, the city had expanded in a number of phases; these corresponded to the regular streets, for example in *Regio* 6. Because he could not identify a symmetrical grid or, even, a semblance of a grid at the site, he rejected the idea that Pompeii was laid out in a single phase. In other words, Pompeii did not entirely conform to Haverfield's expectation that Roman cities should have a symmetrical grid. Therefore, he had to explain this phenomenon and chose a chronological explanation, in which each block of symmetrical streets represented a different phase in the city's expansion. He ignored an alternative explanation, given by Unwin, that the inexactitude of the layout of streets in Pompeii could be accounted for by the way the planner had utilised natural features, such as contours (Unwin 1909: 49; see also Miller 1992). In fact, the layout of Pompeian *insulae* has a close relationship to the natural topography of the site. *Regiones* 1 and 6, the most regular, are upon land that slopes in a southerly direction. The roughly square *insulae*, to the east of Via di Stabia, are built on an area of ground sloping to the south. *Regio* 8 is dominated by its topography, with streets following the contours of the site. *Regio* 7 displays an irregular pattern, but this may be caused by the pressure on space in this central area. This may have altered the original street pattern. Such a view would not have harmonised with Haverfield's notion of the ancients' strict adhesion to a geometric system of planning. As a result, Haverfield was forced to suggest that the area around the forum was an earlier (uncivilised) prehistoric settlement and that, from this area, the city expanded in a systematic (civilised) fashion. In doing so, he had in mind the modern schemes for the expansion of cities such as Barcelona. He used the same terminology, referring to this area as the *Altstädt*: a view accepted by some to this day (Ling 1991: 253; Carocci *et al.* 1990: 207). There is little real evidence for Haverfield's chronology of town extension in Pompeii (De Caro 1985; Chiaramonte Trerè 1986: 16–19; Sakai 1991: 38). Therefore, in the absence of an archaeological chronology for the development of the site, Haverfield adapted the modern notion of town planning to the AD 79 evidence.

This interpretation of the evidence provided a historical justification for twentieth-century planning. Also, in many ways, his work gave the ancient city builder the rationality of the twentieth-century planner, with little account of other factors such as topography. This view of town planning as a geometric grid was outdated by 1913. Geddes' methods of a thorough city survey, displayed at the Cities and Town Planning Exhibition, 1911, giving an account of geography, history, sociology, biology, engineering, aesthetics and architecture, revealed the complexity of town planning in reality, as compared to the drawing-office version based upon geometry (Meller 1990: 157). The complex reality of town planning did not concern Haverfield, who ardently stated that geometry was the key to a civilised urban society similar to that of the Roman Empire.

In the same year as the Town Planning Conference, 1910, Adshead, the first Professor of Town Planning, explained the implications of the Town Planning Act of 1909 in the new journal *Town Planning Review*. He saw planning not only as a means of defining traffic routes, providing parks,

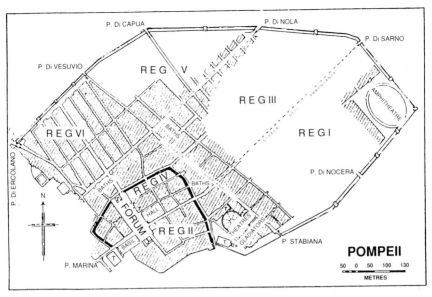

(T = Temple. The area of the supposed original settlement is outlined in black.)

Figure 1.1 Haverfield's Pompeii

buildings, factories and commercial zones, but also as a means to stifle socio-economic problems (Dowdall and Adshead 1910: 39–45). Adshead summarises the planner's dilemma:

> The problem of arranging the juxtaposition of the classes or for their separation will constantly present itself, and whilst absolute separation is a policy to be avoided, as being contrary to the natural dependence of the classes upon each other, at the same time to throw them indiscriminately together would be too radical a policy and would most certainly fail.
>
> (Dowdall and Adshead 1910: 50)

What is clear from Adshead's analysis is that, from 1909, the local authorities became interested in planning socio-economic zones in their cities. These zones separated the working class from the middle class, residential areas from industrial areas, etc. In many ways, this is the origin of the urban formations we experience today. These formations had not existed prior to the twentieth century's concern for planning.

The analysis of the city in twentieth-century geography has concentrated upon the definition of economic zoning from empirical evidence. The studies which have resulted have produced a number of models of the city. The most influential of these models are the concentric zone and Hoyt's

17

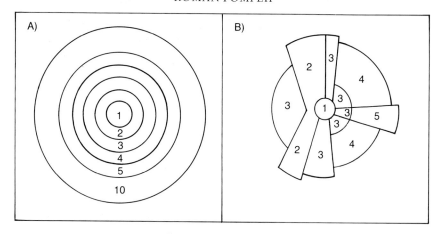

1   Central business district
2   Wholesale light manufacturing
3   Low-class residential
4   Medium-class residential
5   High-class residential
6   Heavy manufacturing
7   Outlying business district
8   Residential suburb
9   Industrial suburb
10 Commuters' zone

Figure 1.2 Models of zoning in the modern city:
A) The concentric-zone model; B) The sectorial model

sectorial model. The concentric-zone model views the city as arranged around a central core containing the government and administrative buildings, and the main business area. This area is termed the Central Business District (CBD). Around the CBD, there are a series of concentric zones. The first and second are areas of light manufacturing and wholesaling, the third low-class housing, the fourth middle-class housing, the fifth high-class housing and the sixth out of town manufacturing (Ayeni 1979: 12). In this model, the socio-economic status of residents increases as the distance from the centre increases. The second model, Hoyt's sectorial model, assumes there is a CBD, but suggests that the city is zoned in sectors, according to urban land rents. The zones tend to be associated with transport corridors radiating from the CBD (Ayeni 1979: 12–13). The usefulness of these economic models of the city is limited for the study of Pompeii. Pompeii does not exhibit any traits of socio-economic zoning (Raper 1977). As is argued below, no single social group was confined to, or desired to live, in a separate area of the city segregated from the rest of society. However, the observation that the city clusters around a central CBD may be of some use. In Pompeii, we might be able to identify the

18

forum as the central core around which the city was arranged. The forum was the area in which the administrative, religious, political, symbolic, economic and social functions of the city were concentrated. Also, there was a series of streets that radiated from the forum to the city gates, which formed transport corridors to Pompeii's rural hinterland. However, Pompeii does not appear to have been arranged according to economic zoning, in which the elite were separated from the rest of society. Such economic zoning only appears in cities that have experienced the Euro-American Industrial Revolution in the nineteenth century and Euro-American planning law in the twentieth century (Ayeni 1979: 11–33). Pompeii, then, does not easily fit modern concepts of land use and spatial division.

To begin to understand the nature of urban space in Pompeii, we need to recognise what we are dealing with. The relationship between urban space and society in Pompeii was complex and cannot neatly fit any one single theory (Lefebvre 1991; Harvey 1988; Castells 1977 address this problem in the modern city). The built environment of Pompeii was a product of Pompeian society (Harvey 1988: 196). By studying urban space in Pompeii, we are examining the social relationships and social choices of Pompeian society in space (Soja 1989: 76–93). Therefore, through the analysis of urban space in Pompeii, we come to understand the underlying social structure of Pompeian society.

The relationship between space and society is complex. Urban space in Pompeii reflects the nature of Pompeian society. However, we need to recognise that space is not entirely a neutral commodity (see Hillier and Hanson 1984 for a theory of urban space). Individuals were born not only in an urban environment that had already been constructed. Their social choices were made in the context of this urban environment. Moreover, urban space has its own structure and rules: it cannot be arranged in a totally random way. Buildings have to be entered from the street and require an independent entrance for the inhabitants' sole use. Also, the arrangement of the streets is a factor in the non-random structure of space. This would have been a factor at Pompeii. The emphasis upon private property had an effect upon the arrangement of space. This feature of Pompeian society placed a constraint upon the arrangement of space. Equally, the preferences of individuals, the concentration or aggregation of activities, the through-put of people and the ideology of Pompeian society all place their own constraints upon the randomness of space. In effect, it is the urban society that alters the random nature of space and moulds space to its needs. In effect, Pompeii and the urban space it contains were social products rather than planned entities.

2

PUBLIC BUILDING AND URBAN IDENTITY

The public buildings in a Roman city were the most prominent features that would have been noted by a visitor to the city. For example, when Pausanias described Panopeus, he did not wish to describe the settlement as a *polis*, because it lacked public buildings (Pausanias 10.4). Therefore, public buildings were considered to be important: more than that, they created an identity for the inhabitants. Above all, they reflected the needs of the population with respect to the gods. Most public buildings were associated with a religious aspect, whether they were temples, theatres, amphitheatres, basilicas or *macella* (markets). However, there is also a secular dimension to these buildings. Their construction by an individual enhanced that person's prestige and position in society (Veyne 1990: 10–12). Their name was clearly displayed upon the structure. The public buildings, as monuments, offered each inhabitant of Pompeii an image of their position in relationship to the power of others, the state and the gods (Lefebvre 1991: 220–2). For example, a temple would have exalted a god and the builder of the temple, and emphasised the social distance and divisions of the community (Lefebvre 1991: 220; Scheid 1992). This makes monuments very different from domestic structures. They take on roles that express the power, the ideology and the identity of a society, and in doing so, they express values that are timeless and associated with tradition (Rossi 1982: 22). In Pompeii, the construction of public buildings is an expression of the identity and the ideology of the inhabitants from the early colony until the city's destruction in AD 79.

Pompeii was a Roman colony from, at the latest, 80 BC (Mouritsen 1988: 71; cf. Castrén 1975: 49–54). The settlement of Sullan veterans alongside the existing inhabitants of the city caused conflict and change (App., *B.C.* 2.94; Cic., *Sull.* 60–1). The period of the early colony saw a fundamental restructuring of monumental space to account for the needs of the new community. When the colony was founded, there were already several large temples, a bath building, a theatre, a basilica, a *macellum* and a forum complex.[1] The public buildings of Pompeii would have been viewed by those arriving in the city. The visitor would have been aware of the prominent Doric temple in

20

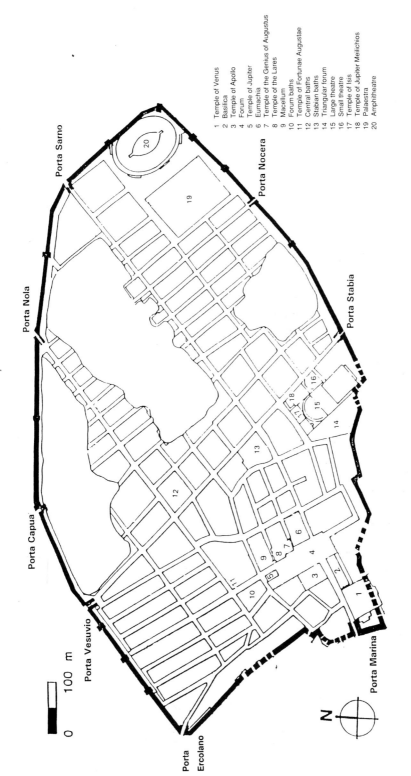

1 Temple of Venus
2 Basilica
3 Temple of Apollo
4 Forum
5 Temple of Jupiter
6 Eumachia
7 Temple of the Genius of Augustus
8 Temple of the Lares
9 Macellum
10 Forum baths
11 Temple of Fortunae Augustae
12 Central baths
13 Stabian baths
14 Triangular forum
15 Large theatre
16 Small theatre
17 Temple of Isis
18 Temple of Jupiter Meilichios
19 Palaestra
20 Amphitheatre

Map 2.1 The public buildings

Porta Sarno

Porta Nola

Porta Capua

Porta Vesuvio

Porta Ercolano

Porta Nocera

Porta Stabia

Porta Marina

0   100 m

N

Plate 2.1 The temple of Apollo

the triangular forum rising above the city walls as they arrived at Pompeii's port on the river Sarno (see Sogliano 1901; Della Corte 1928; Fienga 1932/3 on archaeological evidence). When the visitor entered the city via the Porta Marina, they would have become aware of the temple of Apollo. Once in the forum, the visitor would have seen the recently completed basilica and *macellum*,[2] and the shops opening on to the eastern side of the forum (Maiuri 1973: 53–125). From the forum, the visitor would have seen the Stabian baths on Via dell'Abbondanza. Finally there was the theatre, in close proximity to the triangular forum, for the holding of plays at festivals. This would have given the visitor an impression of the city and its inhabitants. The impression was one of a Hellenistic city, with some attributes of Roman culture, such as the basilica (Zanker 1988a: 5–18). This image was to be altered fundamentally once the colony had been established.

The settlement of a large number of veterans in Pompeii alongside the existing inhabitants caused a certain amount of conflict. The nature of this conflict has been a matter of controversy. Cicero stated in his speech in defence of Publius Sulla (*Pro Sulla* 61) that there had been a quarrel between the new settlers and the Pompeians over *suffragium* and *ambulatio* (Castrén 1975: 82–92; Wiseman 1977; Mouritsen 1988: 71–9; Andreau 1980). The issue of *suffragium* would appear to refer to the constitution imposed by the founders of the colony. Naturally, the *Colonia Cornelia Veneria Pompeianorum* was set up with a Roman political organisation (see Castrén 1975: 55–79 on magistrates). There was an *ordo* of elected *duumviri* and annually elected aediles. In this constitution, the existing inhabitants were not excluded from office holding or voting (Mouritsen 1988: 85–9; contra Castrén 1975: 82–92). It was the nature of the constitution that caused the disagreement between the existing inhabitants and new colonists. There is little evidence for the notion that the inhabitants lost the franchise or for the existence of two sets of magistrates in Pompeii, one for the colonists and one for the existing inhabitants. At the same time the city was divided into *vici* (wards) with altars to the *Lares Compitales* sited at the *compita* or crossroads (*CIL* 4.60 records a list of magistrates from 47/46 BC). This created new local areas with magistrates to celebrate festivals at the local shrines, a parallel for which can be found at Rome with the celebration of the *Compitalia* by the *magistri vici* (Jongman 1988: 295–300; Mouritsen 1990; Laurence 1991; Flambard 1977, 1981). The other issue of contention for the Pompeians was an *ambulatio* (a covered building similar to a *porticus*).[3] This would appear to have been a new structure in Pompeii, and might refer to a structure close to the theatre, or to the Porticus of Vibius in the forum (Wiseman 1977; Richardson 1988: 145–7). The issue may have been that land had been expropriated for the construction of the *ambulatio*, or that its construction was in such a way that it altered the nature of space to cause offence to the Pompeians. The quarrel was healed by the intervention of Publius Sulla, one of the patrons of the colony (Cic., *Sull.* 60–61: on patrons of the colony see Castrén 1975: 56; Harmand 1957: 24, 88–100). However, perhaps we should not take Cicero's statements too literally. After all, he was attempting to defend Publius Sulla rather than to describe accurately the topography of Pompeii.

It was in this period, after the founding of the colony, that the structure of monumental space was fundamentally altered (here I follow Zanker 1988a: 18–25). The forum was developed to reflect the needs and demands of the new settlers. At the north end of the forum the temple of Jupiter was established (Richardson 1988: 138–45; Maiuri 1973: 101–24; Mau 1899: 63–9). This temple was the dominant focus for those using the forum. At the southern end of the forum, a *porticus* was constructed behind which there were three public buildings (see *CIL* 10.794 on the *porticus*). These are commonly associated with the magistrates of the city: one for the two *duumviri*, one for the aediles and one for the meetings of the *ordo* (Zanker 1988a: fig. 12). It seems more likely that these three buildings were for the government of the city, and they may conform to Vitruvius' (5.2) ideals for the placement of buildings in the forum. He states that the treasury, the

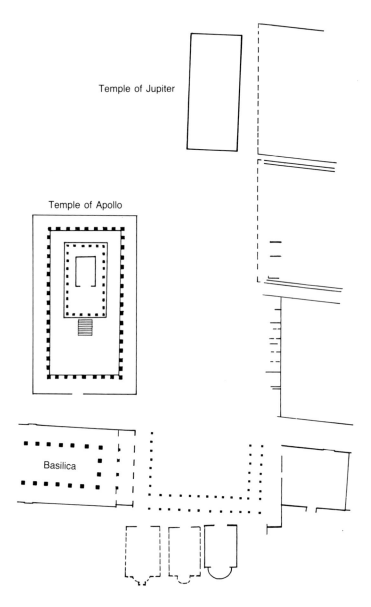

Temple of Jupiter

Temple of Apollo

Basilica

Figure 2.1 The forum in the republic (after Zanker 1988a)

Plate 2.2 The temple of Jupiter

prison and the *curia* should all be sited in the forum. These three unident-ified buildings in Pompeii can be associated with these civic functions, which would have been a necessary part of the structure of the colony. Finally, in the south-eastern corner of the forum, another public building was con-structed that is commonly identified as the *comitium* of the city. This identification is dubious at best (Richardson 1988: 145–7). However, it was an important building in its time; the identification of a functional purpose is now impossible.

Building activity was not confined to the forum. Two *duumviri*, C. Quinctius Valgus and M. Porcius, built the small covered theatre (*CIL* 10.844; Richardson 1988: 131–4; Mau 1899: 153–6). Why there was a need for such a theatre is uncertain. The extant theatre may have been suitable for Greek- or Oscan-style performances and could not be adapted to the needs of the Roman theatre. Therefore, it is possible that this covered theatre was used for Roman-style celebrations, whilst the existing theatre continued to serve the needs of the Oscan community (see Rawson 1985 on Italian influence upon Roman theatre). An alternative explanation is more plausible. The small covered theatre in close proximity to the large theatre

25

may not have been used for the staging of plays at all. The structure has close architectural parallels with structures at Corinth, Argos, Athens and Epidauros, which appear to have been used for the performance of rhetorical exercises or the reading of literary works. It seems likely that the covered theatre at Pompeii would have served a similar purpose in the colonial period. Clearly, it was felt that the performance of rhetoric was a necessary part of the cultural life of the city. Later, as *magistri quinquennales*, C. Quinctius Valgus and M. Porcius built the large amphitheatre to the south-east of the city (*CIL* 10.852; Richardson 1988: 134–8; Mau 1899: 212–26). This structure replaced the forum as the venue for gladiatorial games (see Vitr. 5.1–3 on the use of fora for *munera*). These buildings were important in shaping the community. In the theatre and the amphitheatre, the population of the city and its hinterland sat to watch the games, thus fostering an idea of community and consensus (Lefebvre 1991: 222; Hopkins 1983: 1–30; Rawson 1987). During the games, the conflict within the community of Pompeii would have been forgotten, but not resolved. Also, the identity of the city was altered by the introduction of buildings for Roman-style games, because the celebration of the city's festivals in a new style may have provided a catalyst for acculturation between the colonists and the Pompeians. Further construction of leisure facilities included the building of two new sets of baths: those to the north of the forum and the suburban baths outside the Porta Marina (Richardson 1988: 147–53; Mau 1899: 202–7. On salt-water baths run by M. Crassus Frugus see *CIL* 10.1063; Plin., *N.H.* 31.2.5). Also, the Stabian baths were altered to cater for the colonists' tastes (*CIL* 10.829; Eschebach 1973; Richardson 1988: 100–5). The identity of Pompeii as the *Colonia Cornelia Veneria* was enhanced by the construction of the temple of Venus to the south-west of the city (Zanker 1988a: 19–22; Mau 1899: 124–9). The temple replaced earlier houses and encroached upon Via Marina (Arthur 1986: 38). The temple rose high above the city walls and would have been a prominent focus for visitors arriving at the port on the river Sarno. Significantly, the Doric temple in the triangular forum was in a ruinous state during this period (Richardson 1974; Richardson 1988: 73 is supported by a decline in votive offerings in the first century BC. See also D'Ambrosio and Borriello 1990. Contra Ling 1991: 254). It might be suggested that this was not a coincidence. Previously the visitor's attention was drawn to this Doric temple; now their attention was focused upon the temple of Venus close to the Porta Marina. Thus the building and position of the temple of Venus were not accidental: they reflected the new identity of Pompeii as *Colonia Cornelia Veneria Pompeianorum*. When the visitor to the city entered via the Porta Marina, they would have passed the temple of Apollo and entered the forum, where their view would have been dominated by the new temple of Jupiter. The visitor was now presented with a higher level of amenities in the city: there were three sets of baths to choose from, two theatres to attend, and a new amphitheatre. Thus, in the period of the early colony, the number of public buildings had doubled in a process of cultural accumulation and change. The colonists' needs were met through the construction of public buildings grafted on to the extant buildings in Pompeii. This resulted in a mixture of new and old that provided an identity for both the colonist and the Pompeian. Within a generation, this identity would have no longer reflected the divisions between the colonists and the Pompeians. Cicero, in the *Pro Sulla* (61–2), noted that Publius Sulla, a patron of the colony, had resolved the differences between the colonists and the Pompeians, and that both colonists and Pompeians were in the court room in his support in 62 BC. Therefore, by the end of the first century BC, the inhabitants of Pompeii were united, as a single community with an array of public monuments that reflected the city's status as a Roman colony.

The imperial period saw further development of public buildings throughout the city. Many of these projects mirrored the imperial building programmes at Rome (Zanker 1988a: 26–40, 1988b: 297–334 on this subject).

Plate 2.3 The amphitheatre

27

Unlike the public buildings in the capital, the initiative for certain styles and types of building was not selected by the emperor or his minions. It was the individual sponsor of a project, who determined the style and nature of the building. In many ways, these buildings reflect the new ideology of consensus under the rule of the emperor.

It was in the forum that the influence of the emperor was most strongly felt. The shops on the eastern side of the forum were demolished to make way for a series of public buildings. A *porticus* was built by Eumachia, a public priestess. The *porticus* was dedicated to *Concordia Augusta* and *Pietas* (*CIL* 10.810–12. Richardson 1978 for comparison with Rome; see also Richardson 1988: 194–8; Moeller 1975). The niches at the front of the *porticus* contained images of famous men from Roman history: Aeneas leaving Troy (*CIL* 10.808) and Romulus, the founder of Rome (*CIL* 10.809). Significantly, the inscription for the statue of Romulus is an exact copy of that in the Augustan forum in Rome (Richardson 1988: 194). Many scholars have sought parallels between this building and the *porticus* of Livia at Rome, which was dedicated to *Concordia Augusta*, built in 7 BC (amongst others Richardson 1978; Zanker 1988b: 320–3). However, the *porticus* of Livia as it appears on the *Forma Urbis* has little in common with the *porticus* built by Eumachia in terms of architectural plan, apart from the fact that both buildings have an apse (Rodriguez-Almeida 1980). The buildings were both dedicated to *Concordia Augusta*, and the additional feature of the statues of famous men in the *porticus* of Eumachia in Pompeii has parallels with the ideology of the Augustan capital. The function of this large *porticus* has been hotly debated (Moeller 1976: 57–71; Jongman 1988: 179–84). However, perhaps we should not be too eager to identify such buildings with utilitarian purposes, especially not with a single function that excludes all others. A *porticus* could have been utilised for a number of purposes. It provided a colonnaded area adjacent to the forum where people could meet, transact business, etc. Therefore, this *porticus* may have been used in the similar way to that of a basilica. According to Vitruvius, a basilica should be sited at a warm spot adjacent to the forum so that the *negotiatores* could meet in the winter (Vitr. 5.1.4). One of the groups of *negotiatores* that met in the *porticus* of Eumachia may have been the fullers, who set up a statue to her at the rear of the *porticus* (*CIL* 10.813). Undoubtedly, the *porticus* of Eumachia was used by other groups and for other purposes as well. However, few of these have made an impression upon the archaeological record. To the north of this *porticus*, the temple of the *Genius* of Augustus was constructed. This temple was constructed by Mamia, a public priestess (*CIL* 10.816). Richardson considers the temple to have been built in the Augustan period (Richardson 1988: 191–4; Mau 1899: 102–5). Certainly, there was an active interest in the worship of Augustus or at least his *Genius* in Pompeii. This included a *flamen* or *sacerdos divi Augusti* and *magistri* and *ministri augusti* (Castrén 1975: 68–9). The building to the north of the

28

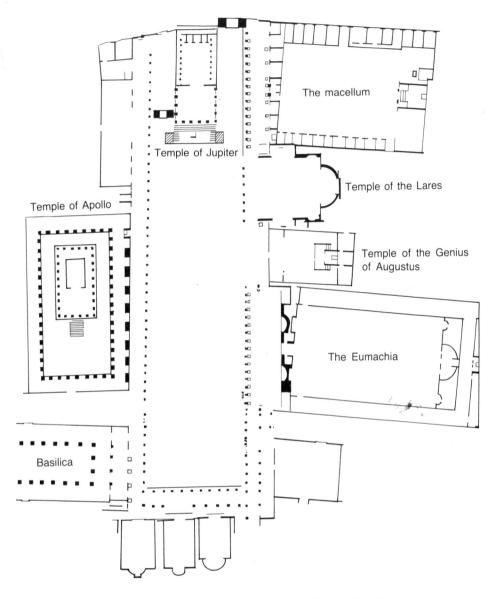

Figure 2.2 The forum in the empire (after Zanker 1988a)

The macellum

Temple of Jupiter

Temple of the Lares

Temple of Apollo

Temple of the Genius of Augustus

The Eumachia

Basilica

temple of the *Genius* of Augustus is difficult to date or identify for any particular purpose. It tends to be associated with a religious function and is known as the temple of the city *Lares*. Most scholars tend to date it to after the earthquake of AD 62 (Richardson 1988: 273–5; Mau 1899: 102–5). Their reasons are that there is no evidence of repair to the building and that they cannot believe that such a complicated structure could have survived intact after the earthquake of AD 62. However, the ability of any building to survive seismic activity depends not upon the simplicity of the structure, but upon how the forces are distributed (for analysis of how earthquakes affect buildings, see Dalby 1972; Verney 1979; Ambrose and Vergun 1980). For example, the use of columns would have caused considerable weakness in a Roman temple; but the temple of the city *Lares* used no columns in its construction. Although the building displays a plan of complexity, it would have been relatively stable during seismic activity. Therefore, it is not impossible that it was built prior to the earthquake of AD 62 (Zanker 1988a: 28 considers it to be Augustan). The building appears to have been dedicated to the worship of the imperial cult, with niches for statues. Indeed, there would appear to have been some architectural parallels between this building and the Pantheon at Rome (Richardson 1988: 274, in particular the floor; he rejects the idea that the building had a domed roof). To the north of the building was the *macellum*, which in the imperial period served as a market for the sale of fish and other perishables (De Ruyt 1983: 141–9; Richardson 1988: 200–1; Mau 1899: 94–101). At the eastern end of the *macellum*, there was a shrine with statues of the imperial family (Zanker 1988a: 28; Richardson 1988: 201). Therefore, on the eastern side of the forum, a *porticus*, a temple of the *Genius* of Augustus, another temple of the imperial cult and the *macellum* were developed in the early imperial period to reflect the position of the emperor in the lives of the inhabitants of Pompeii.

At the same time as the development on the eastern side of the forum, the northern end was also being developed. A series of monumental arches were built in this period. An arch was constructed on either side of the temple of Jupiter. This caused the northern end of the forum to replicate the appearance of the *Forum Romanum* at Rome, where the temple of *Divus Julius* was flanked by monumental arches (Coarelli 1980: 75–6). It is impossible to be sure about the identification and the dating of these arches or to be certain to whom they were dedicated, but it is probable that they commemorated actions of the imperial family (Richardson 1988: 206–9). The effect would have been to enhance the appearance of the *Capitolium* with arches on either side commemorating the achievements of the imperial family. This was complemented by the paving of the forum in Caserta limestone (Richardson 1988: 209–10). In addition, a number of statue bases were erected at the southern end of the forum. Zanker has identified these with the imperial family (Zanker 1988a: 32–3). Therefore, for a person in the forum, to the north there was the *Capitolium* flanked by arches commemorating the

Plate 2.4 The Eumachia

imperial family, on the eastern side there was a series of buildings associated with the imperial cult, and at the southern end there was a series of statues of the emperor and his family. Thus, the forum was transformed from being the cult centre of the city into a religious centre with a strong emphasis on the person and family of the sacrosanct emperor.

It was not only in the forum that building activity took place: to the north, an arch commemorating the imperial family was built. The temple of *Fortunae Augustae* was built opposite the forum baths (Richardson 1988: 202–6; Mau 1899: 130–2). This temple was built in AD 3 by M. Tullius, a *duumvir quinquennalis*, on his own land (*CIL* 10.824 dates the temple; see *CIL* 10.820, 821 on M. Tullius). The temple was constructed so that the worshipper had to stand at an angle of 90 degrees to the street (Vitr. 5.1). This temple seems to have been at the centre of the imperial cult. At the time of its foundation, the first *ministri Fortunae Augustae* were established (*CIL* 10.824: on these *ministri* see Castrén 1975: 76–7 and Mouritsen 1988: 92–9). These minor officials were drawn from the slaves and freedmen of the city. Their activities were concentrated at this temple, where the majority of inscriptions referring to them are found (Castrén 1975: 76).

31

To the west of the forum, the temple of Apollo was remodelled by
M. Holconius Rufus and C. Egnatius Postumus, and a sundial was added
(*CIL* 10.787, 802; Zanker 1988a: 26). The importance of Apollo in Pompeii's
religious calendar is well attested. A. Clodius Flaccus, in his first duumvirate, organised the procession and games of Apollo. The procession held in
the forum included: bulls, bullfighters, various different types of fighters for
the amphitheatre and three troops of boxers. For the games, he funded a
pantomime and put up the money to pay the famous pantomime actor
Pylades (*CIL* 10.1074; Beacham 1991: 140–53. On actors in Pompeii, see
Franklin 1987). The inclusion of Pylades, one of the most famous actors
of the Augustan age, demonstrates the cultural prominence of Pompeii
(on culture see Gigante 1979). As *duumvir*, A. Clodius Flaccus provided
only part of the entertainment for the festival; others would have provided complementary elements. In his second duumvirate, A. Clodius
Flaccus provided, for the same festival, the procession in the forum, as
above, and on the next day a spectacle in the amphitheatre that included:
thirty pairs of athletes, five pairs of gladiators, another thirty-five pairs of

Plate 2.5 Monumental arch north of the forum. The temple of Jupiter is to the left,
and the *macellum* is to the right

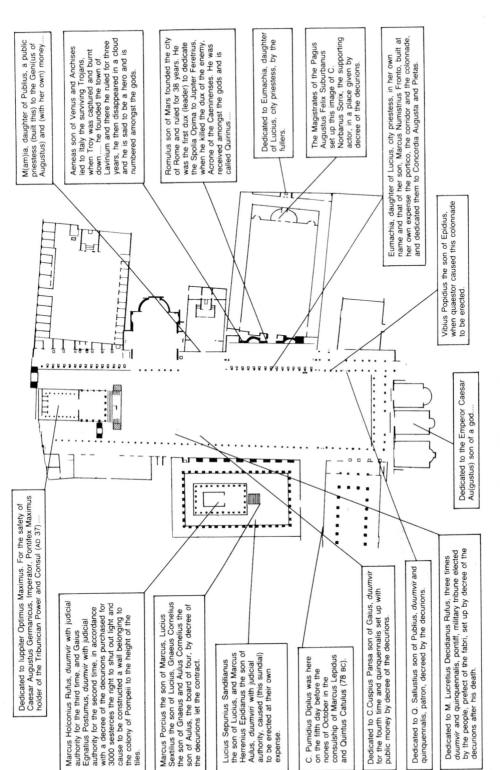

M(am)ia, daughter of Publius, a public priestess (built this) to the Geni(us of Augustus) and (with her own) money....

Aeneas son of Venus and Anchises led to Italy the surviving Trojans, when Troy was captured and burnt down.... he founded the town of Lavinium and there he ruled for three years, he then disappeared in a cloud and he is said to be a hero and is numbered amongst the gods.

Romulus son of Mars founded the city of Rome and ruled for 38 years. He was the first dux (leader) to dedicate the Spolia Opima to Jupiter Feretrius, when he killed the dux of the enemy, Acrone of the Caeninenses. He was received amongst the gods and is called Quirinus.....

Dedicated to Eumachia, daughter of Lucius, city priestess, by the fullers.

The Magistrates of the Pagus Augustus Felix Suburbanus set up this image of C. Norbanus Sorix, the supporting actor, in a place given by decree of the decurions.

Eumachia, daughter of Lucius, city priestess, in her own name and that of her son, Marcus Numistrius Fronto, built at her own expense the portico, the corridor and the colonnade, and dedicated them to Concordia Augusta and Pietas.

Vibius Popidius the son of Epidius, when quaestor caused this colonnade to be erected.

Dedicated to the Emperor Caesar Au(gustus) son of a god....

Dedicated to Iuppiter Optimus Maximus. For the safety of Caesar Augustus Germanicus, Imperator, Pontifex Maximus holder of the Tribunician Power and Consul (AD 37)....

Marcus Holconius Rufus, duumvir with judicial authority for the third time, and Gaius Egnatius Postumus, duumvir with judicial authority for the second time, in accordance with a decree of the decurions purchased for 3000 sesterces the right to shut out light and cause to be constructed a wall belonging to the colony of Pompeii to the height of the tiles.

Marcus Porcius the son of Marcus, Lucius Sextilius the son of Lucius, Gnaeus Cornelius the son of Gnaeus and Aulus Cornelius the son of Aulus, the board of four, by decree of the decurions let the contract.

Lucius Sepunius Sandilianus the son of Lucius, and Marcus Herrenius Epidianus the son of Aulus, duumviri with judicial authority, caused (this sundial) to be erected at their own expense.

C. Pumidius Dipilus was here on the fifth day before the nones of October in the consulship of Marcus Lepidus and Quintus Catulus (78 BC).

Dedicated to C.Cuspius Pansa son of Gaius, duumvir for the fourth time and quinquennalis set up with public money by decree of the decurions.

Dedicated to Q. Sallustius son of Publius, duumvir and quinquennalis, patron, decreed by the decurions.

Dedicated to M. Lucretius Decidianus Rufus, three times duumvir and quinquennalis, pontiff, military tribune elected by the people, prefect of the fabri, set up by decree of the decurions after his death.

Figure 2.3 Some inscriptions in the forum

gladiators, and an animal hunt featuring bulls, bullfighters, wild boars, hares and other animals (*CIL* 10.1074). The festival was clearly a way for the elite to enhance their status and standing in the community (Veyne 1990: 208–34), and the accumulation of ever more elaborate features was the direct result of this competition between them. Finally, the celebration of a festival upon such a grand scale would have brought renown to Pompeii as a centre of culture.

To enhance the performance of these festivals, the large theatre and amphitheatre were refurbished. The theatre was extensively reconstructed and dedicated to Augustus in 1 BC/AD 1 (*CIL* 10.833–42; Zanker 1988a: 33–6; Richardson 1988: 216–18; Mau 1899: 149–50). This prestigious project was financed by M. Holconius Rufus and M. Holconius Celer. It would appear that the rebuilding of the theatre converted it from one suitable for Greek-style games to the recognisably Roman theatre we see today (Zanker 1988b: 325–6). It was in this theatre that the community were seated in a way which reflected the position of each individual in Pompeian society. At the front were the decurions, behind them were the free adult males and at the back were the free adult females and slaves (Rawson 1987). The stage performance commemorated the actions of the gods and ancestors of those watching. The dedication of the theatre to Augustus emphasised to the Pompeians his position in the state. Also the builders of the theatre, M. Holconius Rufus, a patron of the *colonia*, and M. Holconius Celer, a younger relative of the patron of the colony, gained considerable prestige (the inscriptions in the theatre celebrated the careers of M. Holconius Rufus *CIL* 10.833–9 and M. Holconius Celer *CIL* 10.833–5, 840. On the Holconii see Mouritsen 1988: 102; Castrén 1975: 97, 176). The seating in the amphitheatre was substantially rebuilt in stone in the Augustan period. Wedges of seats were constructed at the expense of individual *duumviri* and, in one case, by the *magistri* of the *Pagus Augustus Felix Suburbanus* (*CIL* 10.853–7). The triangular forum was converted into a park with the Doric temple as a historic ruin. It was here that a statue was set up to M. Claudius Marcellus, Augustus' nephew and patron of the colony (*CIL* 10.832). Also, a sundial was set up here by the *duumviri* L. Sepunius Sandilanus and M. Herrenius Epidianus (*CIL* 10.831). Finally the construction of an aqueduct provided fresh clean water for the baths, some private houses, and the public fountains (Eschebach 1980; Richardson 1988: 51–63).

Therefore, in the early imperial period, the image of the emperor and his family was present in nearly all of the public buildings in Pompeii. Many new buildings had been built. It was, predominantly, the *duumviri* who initiated these projects, but leading female priests, such as Eumachia, could also have financed building projects (Zanker 1988b: 320–3). Thus it was the elite who altered the image of Pompeii in this period. For our visitor arriving at the port on the river Sarno, the initial focus was still the temple

AD 62–79 → Period of reconstruction of Pompeii

of Venus, as they approached the city. Once inside the city walls, they passed the temple of Apollo and entered the forum. Here, they would have been dazzled by the *Capitolium* flanked by two monumental arches, the new *porticus*, and temples associated with the imperial cult on the eastern side of the forum and, finally, they would have noted the statues of the imperial household at the southern end of the forum. As they moved through the city, they would have seen the new public fountains and may have visited the baths, which were abundantly supplied with clear water from the new aqueduct. The theatres and amphitheatre would have added to the image of the city. To the visitor, like the contemporary Seneca, Pompeii was now no ordinary city (Sen., *N.Q.* 6.1; compare Tacitus, *Annals* 15.22). Pompeii was a Roman colony with close cultural connections with the capital. The city enhanced its prestigious status by extensive building projects. The position of the Roman emperor in the state was given expression by the builders, which caused the image of the emperor and the imperial family to be present in most locations of public interaction in the city. Just as Augustus could boast that he had found Rome a city of brick and turned it into a city of marble, the Pompeian elite could point to a similar transformation in their own city (Zanker 1988b: 323).

The earthquake on 5 February AD 62 caused considerable damage to the fabric of Pompeii (Sen., *N.Q.* 6 gives a detailed description. On physical damage to Pompeii see Maiuri 1942). Pompeii appears to have been close to the epicentre of this earthquake (Andreau 1984: 40). Other towns were affected: part of Herculaneum was destroyed, parts of Nuceria were damaged, and in Naples private residences were affected, but the public buildings were untouched. Many people fled from Campania according to Seneca (*N.Q.* 6.10). In Pompeii, it was predominantly the public buildings that were most affected: they were the least resistant to seismic activity. Some buildings may have resisted the seismic waves, including the amphitheatre and the theatres.[4] Parts of the city never recovered in the seventeen-year period between AD 62 and 79, when all the public buildings were undergoing reconstruction. Such an extensive project took time and considerable manpower (Andreau 1973). The aqueduct may not have been reconnected to the water system before AD 79 (Maiuri 1942: 90–4; Andreau 1984: 42), so that the city was once again reliant upon deep wells for its water supply. The forum, with its exuberant public architecture, was not in use in AD 79 (Maiuri 1942). The temple of Venus was being rebuilt on a larger scale than before (Richardson 1988: 280; Mau 1899: 124–9) and the temple of Apollo was undergoing reconstruction (De Caro 1986; Döhl and Zanker 1984: 182). The small temple of Jupiter Meilichios on Via di Stabia housed the statues of Jupiter, Juno and Minerva from the *Capitolium* in the forum. The plan for reconstruction was an ambitious one and may have been supervised by the imperial authorities in the Flavian period (Andreau 1984:

41). After all, it was in this period that T. Suedius Clemens, a Roman tribune, redefined the *pomerium* of the city (cippi, stone markers, record this: CIL 10.10.1018; Conticello 1990: 225; Fiorelli 1875: 404; D'Ambrosio and De Caro 1983: 25; Della Corte 1913; *NS* 1910: 399–401). Little of the restoration work had been completed by AD 79. The temple of Isis had been completely rebuilt, by N. Popidius Celsinus, who was adlected into the *ordo* of decurions for this service at the unusually early age of 6 (*CIL* 10.846; Richardson 1988: 281–5; Döhl and Zanker 1984: 182–5). A new set of baths was being built at the junction of Via di Stabia and Via di Nola (Richardson 1988: 286–9). This new set of baths encroached upon Vicolo di Tesmo to the east, and a street shrine was incorporated into the wall of the building. In the mean time, the inhabitants used the forum baths, which were supplied from cisterns and wells (Zanker 1988a: 42). For our visitor arriving at the port on the river Sarno little of any note rose above the line of the city wall. Now they entered the city via the Porta di Stabia. They may have noted the statues of Jupiter, Juno and Minerva in the temple of Jupiter Meilichios on their way up Via di Stabia. Apart from the new temple of Isis and the amphitheatre, the city was undergoing reconstruction. However, any visitor would have admired the plans of the Pompeians not just to restore their city to its former glory but to rebuild it on an even grander scale.

The urban identity of Pompeii underwent considerable change in the period from 80 BC to AD 79. In the early years of the colony, the existing public buildings were complemented by the construction of new features to provide for the needs of the colonists. This doubled the number of temples, baths and theatres, and an amphitheatre was constructed. In the Augustan and early imperial period, the public buildings of the city were transformed to reflect the emperor's position in the state. Further buildings were added, which caused Pompeii to become one of the prominent cities in Campania. However, in AD 62, disaster struck: most of the public buildings were damaged by earth tremors. The plan for reconstructing the city's public buildings, on a grander scale, was in its infancy when the city was destroyed in AD 79.

In this process of change, the urban elite were motivated to put up buildings to glorify the gods, their city and themselves. In this process of *euergetism*, the elite made choices about what sort of building to put up. For example, Eumachia chose to build a *porticus* dedicated to *Concordia Augusta* and *Pietas*, rather than a temple, theatre or amphitheatre. However, there would seem to have been a practical constraint upon this process. Once a city had one amphitheatre, it would not necessarily have been desirable to have another. Therefore, in the period from 80 BC to AD 79, we see *euergetism* as a cumulative process, in which the civic identity is altered and changed through the addition of new buildings and the restoration and enhancement of the existing structures. This process closely parallels civic developments at Rome. However, in the Augustan period, at Pompeii the

Plate 2.6 The temple of Jupiter Meilichios

commemoration of the emperor's position was not regulated as it was in the capital. In terms of cultural identity, Pompeii was not a backwater, but a Roman colony with strong cultural connections with Rome, the generator of power and cultural ideology.

3

LOCAL IDENTITY: NEIGHBOURS AND NEIGHBOURHOODS

The terms 'neighbours' and 'neighbourhood' are used frequently in any discussion of the modern city. The city is often viewed as composed of a series of local communities, each with its own identity, which are centred upon a particular neighbourhood. In this conception of the city, each neighbourhood is spatially defined and perceived as a separate entity. However, the term 'neighbourhood', like 'community', is notorious for the variety of meanings attached to it (Bulmer 1986: 17). Some definition of the terminology used in this chapter is necessary. Neighbours are simply defined as those people who live in close proximity to one another. In contrast, neighbourhood is 'an effectively defined terrain or locality inhabited by neighbours' (Bulmer 1986: 21). This suggests that 'the word neighbourhood has two general connotations: physical proximity to a given object of attention, and intimacy of association among people living in close proximity to one another' (Hawley 1968: 73 quoted in Bulmer 1986: 19). Neighbourhoods and neighbours are examined in this chapter to establish the nature of local identity in Pompeii.

'Neighbourhood' is a term that usually refers to a subset of the city and is identified by a name of a district, such as Hackney in London. In contrast, the word 'neighbour' is associated with those acquaintances and friends known to a person who live in close proximity to that person's home (Porteous 1977: 68–89). Such concepts were not unfamiliar to those living in the Roman world. The word *vicus* (ward) referred to a neighbourhood of the city. Those living in that *vicus* were termed *vicani*. This is not to be confused with the term *vicini*, which refers to neighbours (Mouritsen 1990: 146–7). Some names that appear in the electoral notices of Pompeii (Forenses, Campanienses, Salinienses, Urbulanenses) have been associated, by modern scholars, with the *vici* of the city (*CIL* 4.783, Forenses, *CIL* 4.470, 480, Campanienses, *CIL* 4.128, Salinienses, *CIL* 4.7676, 7706, 7747, Urbulanenses). Three of these names were also names for three of the gates of the city: the Porta Campana, now Porta di Nola, the Porta Saliniensis, now Porta di Ercolano, and the Porta Urbulania, now Porta di Sarno (Castrén 1975: 80; Mouritsen 1988: 67–8). This might suggest that the *vici* were named after the gates of the city.[1] However, it is unlikely that we have a full sample of all the names of the *vici* from our surviving evidence. The correspondence between the names of the gates and the *vici* should not be overstated. The terms cannot be pinned down to any cohesive geographical or social unit, because our evidence is composed of only six electoral notices in four streets (Castrén 1975: 80–2 associates the *vici* with electoral districts and attempts to delimit them on rather spurious grounds). It is rather the historical context of the division of Pompeii into *vici* that provides us with the evidence which begins to address the question of neighbourhood and local identity. When the colony had been set up under Sulla, all the trappings of Roman culture had been grafted on to the existing city. These included the local cult of the *Lares Compitales*, and a division of the city into *vici*, local neighbourhoods, with two magistrates being selected for each *vicus* (*CIL* 4.60 gives a list of *magistri vici et compiti* for 47/46 BC). It is a reasonable assumption that this division of the city into *vici* was modelled on the system in Rome. So, by analysing the relatively abundant literary and epigraphic evidence from the city of Rome, it may be possible to offer a more detailed interpretation of the surviving epigraphic and archaeological evidence for these divisions in Pompeii.

The city of Rome was divided into a number of local units known as *vici*, each with its own pair of magistrates, and cult of the *Lares Compitales* located at key crossroads (on *vici* in Rome see Flambard 1977 and 1981; Laurence 1991). It was at the shrines of the *Lares Compitales* that the *magistri vici* celebrated festivals such as the *Compitalia*. Thus each inhabitant of the city was a member of a *vicus*, which had magistrates and its own local cult of the *Lares Compitales*. This organisation would have provided each individual inhabitant with a sense of identity and place in the city. The *vici* played an important part in politics, and were utilised by Publius Clodius for the organisation of violent demonstrations in the 50s BC (Vanderbroeck 1987). The administrative division of Rome underwent a fundamental review under Augustus: in 7 BC, the city was divided into fourteen *regiones*, which replaced the four existing *regiones* (Suet., *Aug*.30). These *regiones* were utilised for organising the administration of the city (Robinson 1991: 9–13). Further, according to Suetonius, Augustus divided the city into *vici* and magistrates were annually selected by lot in each *vicus* (Suet., *Aug*.30; Dio 55.8 notes that officials had two lictors: Liv. 31.4.5). This is strange: *vici* had existed in Rome prior to this date (e.g. Cic., *Dom*. 54). It would appear that Augustus was altering the spatial configuration of the *vici* to form a new structure that would replace the existing *vici*. Later in 7 BC, Augustus gave the *magistri vici* the images of the *Lares Augusti*.[2] This is known from the excavation of a structure associated with the *magistri vici* close to the Porticus Aemilia (Mancini 1935; Degrassi 1935, 1947). The excavation uncovered a double-sided slab giving details of the annual calendar, a list of consuls from 43 BC, and a list of *magistri vici* from 7 BC, specifically stating that those of 7 BC were the first *magistri vici*. It was to these magistrates that Augustus had given the images of the *Lares Augusti*. The *Lares Augusti* were not a new cult: an inscription refers to their existence in 59 BC (*ILLRP* 200). Not surprisingly, under Augustus they took on a larger role. These *Lares Augusti* were to be placed in the new shrines of the *vici*. Thus, in effect, the new Augustan *vici* associated with the *Lares Augusti* overlie the older *vici* associated with the *Lares Compitales*. It should be stressed that the *Lares Compitales* continued to exist in the city (Suet., *Aug.* 31 refers to Augustan revival of *Ludi Compitales*). The census for AD 73 recorded 265 of them (Plin., *N.H.* 3.66). The revived cult of the *Lares Augusti* eventually overtook the cult of the *Lares Compitales*. Also, the original division of Rome into *vici* was forgotten in favour of the Augustan division of the city into *regiones* and *vici* (Suet., *Aug.* 30).[3] In Augustan Rome, local identity was centred upon the new division of the city into *vici* and the new cult of the *Lares Augusti*.

If we can identify any evidence that such social processes occurred in Pompeii, we can begin to understand the spatial division of the city that formed the basis for an inhabitant's local identity. Epigraphic evidence for the *vici* of Pompeii is not abundant. A single inscription refers to a list of *magistri vici et compiti* for the years 47 or 46 BC (*CIL* 4.60). This would suggest that Pompeii, like Rome, was divided into *vici*, with magistrates who oversaw the shrines of the *compita* (crossroads) in the republic. Evidence for a reorganisation of this structure, in 7 BC, is derived from a small number of inscriptions referring to the *Pagus Augustus Felix Suburbanus* (*CIL* 10.924, 814, 853, 1042, 1074; Mouritsen 1988: 94; Castrén 1975: 275–6). We know that the first *ministri* of this *pagus* were established in 7 BC, the same year that the *magistri vici* were set up in Rome (*CIL* 10.924). Epigraphic evidence also establishes that this *pagus* had *magistri Augusti*, as well as *ministri Augusti* (*CIL* 10.814, 853, 1042, 1074). I think we may assume that these were established in 7 BC. An epitaph found on a tomb outside the Porta Herculensis (*CIL* 10.1042) was set up to M. Arrius Diomedes, a *magister* in the *Pagus Augustus Felix Suburbanus*. Underneath the inscription were two carved *fasces* representing the emblems of office. Significantly, in Rome, the *magistri vici* were permitted to have two lictors carrying *fasces* (Dio 55.8; Liv. 31.4.5). It would seem that in Pompeii these *magistri Augusti* also had the *fasces* carried before them as emblems of their office. Therefore, we have evidence for the reorganisation or establishment of the *Pagus Augustus Felix Suburbanus* in 7 BC. This would have been a division of the city's territory close to Pompeii. The *pagus* is well represented epigraphically, unlike other *pagi* and *vici* of Pompeii (but see De Franciscis 1976). However, given the nature of the evidence for the *Pagus Augustus Felix Suburbanus* and how it mirrors the reorganisation of the *vici* at Rome, I think that we can infer that a similar reorganisation of the *vici* and the other *pagi* of Pompeii did occur in 7 BC.[4]

Plate 3.1 Street shrine at the north-west corner of *Insula* 9.8

This reorganisation of the *vici* should be relected in the archaeological remains of Pompeii. There are a number of altars found at the cross-roads of streets in Pompeii. The majority of these altars include paintings of the *Lares* above them (Spinazzola 1953: 163–85; Fröhlich 1991). They may also include scenes of sacrifice and images of other gods and serpents.[5] The distribution pattern of these altars in the city raises the question of whether the altar was at the centre of a *vicus*. If so, some of these *vici* would be extremely small units of only a few households. More likely, since most of the altars were sited on the major through-routes of the city, they may have been the markers of a boundary between two *vici*. For example, those along Via dell'Abbondanza would have been visible to anyone entering the city at Porta di Sarno as they moved towards the forum. These altars may have defined the linear perimeter between one *vicus* to the south and another *vicus* to the north of Via dell'Abbondanza. The electoral notices mentioning the *Urbulanenses* all appear on the north side of Via dell'Abbondanza (*CIL* 4.7676 at 3.4.1; *CIL* 4.7706 at 3.4.3; *CIL* 4.7747 at 3.6.1). There is also a very fragmentary list of magistrates from the *vicus Urbulanenses* at 9.7.1 (*CIL* 4.7807; see Jongman 1988: 304–6,

41

which should be read with the critique by Mouritsen 1990). None of the altars of the *Lares* from Pompeii included an image of the *Genius* of Augustus (Mau 1899: 233). Therefore, it is possible that these altars were dedicated to the *Lares Compitales* after the founding of the colony in the republic. It should be noted that some of the altars had fallen into disuse. For example, the altar at the south-east corner of *Insula* 9.4 was incorporated into the rear wall of the central baths. Other altars may have been removed, which might explain the uneven distribution of altars in the city. In the Augustan period, in Rome, the *magistri vici* had been presented with two images of the *Lares Augusti*. These images would appear to have been kept in a central shrine, like that excavated close to the Porticus Aemilia (Mancini 1935). In effect, at Rome, the altars of the *Lares Compitales* were being overshadowed by the centralised cult of the *Lares Augusti*.[6] In Pompeii, there is some evidence for these centralised shrines of the *Lares Augusti*. The structure at 6.1.13 is architecturally similar to the shrine of the *Lares Augusti* excavated near the Porticus Aemilia at Rome (Fiorelli 1875: 81; Degrassi 1935; Mancini 1935). There are two other structures that can also be associated with this cult (6.8.14 and 8.4.24, Fiorelli 1875: 122, 343; Mau 1899: 235). The *Lares Augusti* did not replace the *Lares Compitales*. However, in the first century AD, there was a tendency for people to associate more strongly with the *Lares Augusti* rather than the *Lares Compitales*, which may have caused some altars of the *Lares Compitales* to have been neglected or even removed. Therefore, in Pompeii, we are seeing this process of transition, in which the identity of the inhabitants of each *vicus* became concentrated upon the centralised shrine of the *Lares Augusti* rather than the altars of the *Lares Compitales* that marked the boundaries of the pre-Augustan *vici* of their ancestors. This would suggest that in Augustan Pompeii, the shape of urban space was fundamentally altered with respect to the *vici* and the inhabitants' local identity.

There are a number of electoral notices in which the *vicini* or neighbours recommend candidates for office (Mouritsen 1988: 176). Mouritsen (1988: 146) has pointed out that there are thirty-two in total, which represent 7 per cent of all such recommendations. In the eight cases where a candidate's house can be identified with certainty, there appears to be some correlation between the place of a candidate's residence and the recommendation of that candidate by his *vicini*. However, only one commendation by *vicini* was posted close to a candidate's residence (Mouritsen 1988:19). Therefore, the limited nature of the evidence of electoral notices referring to *vicini* does not enable us to define any particular local area with any certainty. However, the recommendation of a candidate by the *vicini* does highlight the fact that there was a common identity amongst neighbours. These electoral notices play upon the loyalty of neighbours to act in unison.

Neighbourhoods can be recognised through an examination of the provision of public fountains (Jansen 1991; Nishida 1991: 91–8; Eschebach 1979;

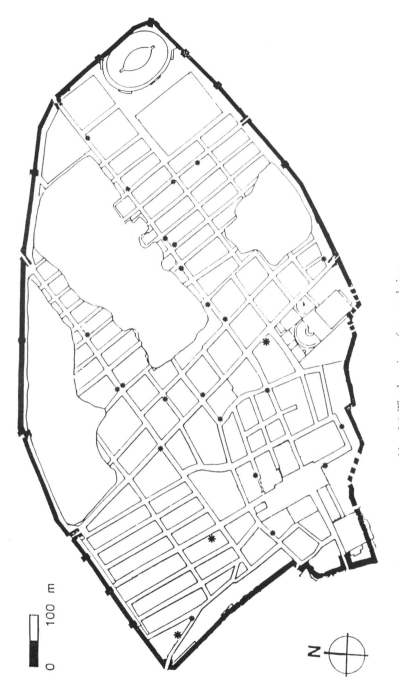

Map 3.1 The location of street shrines

Eschebach and Schäfer 1983; Mygind 1917 and 1921 provide detailed evidence). These fountains would have been used by people in close proximity to them and provided a point of contact between neighbours.[7]

The fountains are considered to be Augustan in date (Richardson 1988: 51–63; Zanker 1988a: 38–40), and were associated with the building of Pompeii's aqueduct. Unlike those elsewhere, Pompeii's aqueduct was built to supply high-quality drinking water, rather than to supply water to new sets of bath buildings (Coulton 1987: 82). Also, the aqueduct would have provided for the existing demands for water: for the baths, private houses and public supplies. This replaced an earlier system utilising wells and cisterns in the city (see Richardson 1988: 51–3 for wells), as can be seen graphically at a crossroads in Via delle Consolare. The deep well behind the fountain was filled up with a deposit that included pottery, lamps and other items. This evidence provided an Augustan date for the fill. As the well had been replaced by the fountain, we can assume that the fountain and, by inference, the aqueduct are Augustan (Richardson 1988: 56; NS 1910: 563–7). This suggests either that something was fundamentally wrong with the water supply from wells or that there was a new demand for good-quality water that led the city of Pompeii to undertake the vast expense of building an aqueduct. There was a cultural demand for good clean aqueduct-borne water in Augustan Italy. Vitruvius (De Architectura 8) has a long discussion about the supply of water to cities and, in particular, drinking water.[8] Vitruvius is quite specific that water from the plains and low-lying regions was of poor quality. However, sources in the mountains and, especially, in forests away from the sun were more suitable (Vitr. 1.7). Later, another author, Frontinus, was preoccupied with the provision of clear drinking water to the people of Rome.[9] He is emphatic that good-quality water should be reserved for drinking, whereas poor-quality water was more suitable for the baths, fulling and other uses (Front., Aqu. 2.92). In Augustus' reign the supply of water to the city of Rome had increased by 78 per cent according to Frontinus' figures (Front., Aqu. 2.65–71).[10] The Augustan date of Pompeii's aqueduct might suggest that, as with many other public-building projects in Pompeii at this time, we might be seeing a desire to imitate developments in Rome and provide good-quality drinking water (compare Front., Aqu. 1.24).

The supply of water to Pompeii is strikingly similar to Vitruvius' description of how it should be done (8.6). The water arrived in the city at a castellum (reservoir) at the highest point in the city. In the castellum the water was divided into three, with one of these divisions receiving significantly more water; water left the castellum in three large pipes. Vitruvius suggests (8.6.2) that: the central pipe, which received more water, should be for the pools and fountains of the city; a second pipe was for the baths, which provided the city with revenue; and a third pipe provided water to private users who would pay for its use. Clearly

Plate 3.2 A fountain in Via della Fortuna

Plate 3.3 An Augustan fountain has been placed in front of an altar at the junction of Via delle Consolare and Vicolo di Narciso. Note the well head behind the altar

45

Plate 3.4 The *castellum* at Porta Vesuvio. Note the three pipes leaving the *castellum*

Vitruvius considered that the supply of water to fountains and pools should be at least one-third or even half of the total amount of water delivered to the city by the aqueduct. This suggests that many people in the Roman cities in the first century AD utilised a public supply of water. In Pompeii, many of the houses had their own internal water supply. However, this supply might not have fulfilled all their needs for water and, even where a house had its own supply, water may have also been collected from a public fountain.[11]

To turn to the spatial distribution of fountains in Pompeii, these were nearly always located at a street junction. Very few were located to supersede known sites of deep wells. What is most striking about the location of both fountains and water towers is the way in which they caused obstruction in certain streets. In some cases they even prevented access to wheeled traffic, and the fountain in Via delle Consolare obscured an altar of the *Lares Compitales*. The engineer who established the public fountains faced restrictions in their locations. Where there was space, they were located close to local shrines. However, in the narrower streets, they were placed in a manner that least impeded movement through the streets. In some cases, the

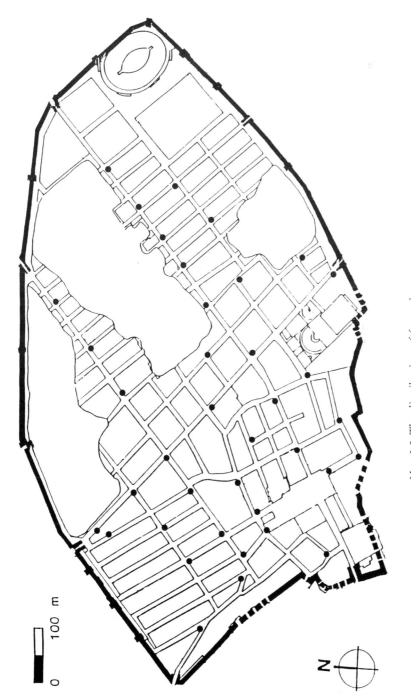

Map 3.2 The distribution of fountains

0   100 m

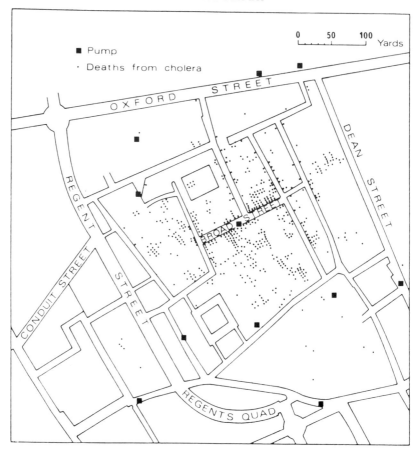

Map 3.3 John Snow's map of the cholera outbreak in Broad Street (1854)

fountain actually blocked the street, because the fountains were located so that they did not encroach upon private property. This might suggest that their location was not sympathetic to the existing patterns of social activity and water collection. Indeed, the establishment of public fountains may have altered the existing pattern of social activity at a local level within the city.

People utilising a public water supply tend to draw their water from the nearest source, particularly if water in the city is of a standard quality. This can be illustrated with reference to Snow's study of an outbreak of cholera in Soho in 1854. There were 500 fatalities in a period of ten days.[12] Snow succeeded in locating the source of the outbreak to a single pump in Broad Street. His method of locating it was simple: he plotted the mortalities on a map. This provided him with the spatial distribution of cholera victims, which was clustered around the pump in Broad Street (Snow 1965: 38–55;

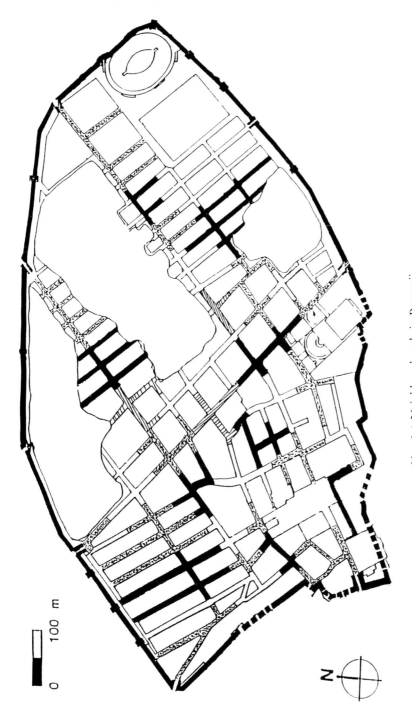

Map 3.4 Neighbourhoods in Pompeii

Pelling 1978). For our purposes, Snow's distribution map of fatalities from cholera provides an expected pattern of use of a water supply. Use was localised, with a number of people travelling to Broad Street to collect water from further afield, because the Broad Street pump delivered good-tasting water, unlike the pump in Carnaby Street, which no one used (Snow 1965: 46). In the case of Pompeii, such a discrepancy should not arise, because all fountains were supplied with water of the same quality, from the *castellum* of the aqueduct. If anything, the pattern of use should be more localised. To reconstruct the pattern of use for the fountains of Pompeii, each fountain was plotted on a base map; then the distance between each fountain and the next was measured: the mid point of this distance was seen to be the edge of the area associated with those drawing water from a specific fountain. The assumption was that a person used the nearest fountain. This process was repeated for all fountains and was plotted as Map 3.4. The shaded areas on the map represent the local areas that utilised each fountain. The local pattern of water collection is similar to Snow's pattern of fatalities from cholera in 1854. Most people in Pompeii lived within 80 metres of a fountain. The local areas that used individual fountains would have been relatively small, with a number of exceptions to the south-east of the city. There were fewer fountains in this area of lower-density settlement, which might suggest that the density of fountains reflects the public demand for water in the city. Therefore, from the distribution map a series of very localised areas were established, where the inhabitants drew water from the same fountain. These areas might correspond to the localised neighbour-hoods in the city of Pompeii. This pattern of local divisions in the city would have been established by the manner in which the fountains were originally distributed by the designer.

Many features of local identity such as the houses of friends, prominent individuals, patrons and so forth cannot be identified from the archaeological record. However, at a local level an individual in Pompeii would have had a close affinity to their neighbourhood or *vicus*. This was focused upon their local shrine of the *Lares Augusti* and the altars of the *Lares Compitales*. In each of these neighbourhoods, there were two local magistrates. Closer to home, an individual would identify with their neighbours. These forms of local identity existed alongside each other, and were fundamental for the inhabitants to make sense of the city. Their importance as factors of local identity is highlighted by the Augustan reorganisation of the city of Rome. This imperial action was emulated in the reorganisation of space in Pompeii.

4

PRODUCTION
AND CONSUMPTION

The excavations at Pompeii have produced tens of thousands of artefacts, many of them produced locally, but many also coming from other parts of the empire or even beyond. At the same time items produced at or near Pompeii found their way to sites elsewhere. Within the city itself there is plentiful evidence of workshops and market gardening. This raises the questions: what does all this evidence amount to and how should we characterise the economy of Pompeii?

The Roman city has been described as a consumer city (Weber 1958; Finley 1973; Hopkins 1978; Jongman 1988; Whittaker 1990). In this model the city is represented as economically dependent upon the agricultural production of its hinterland. The surplus wealth from this agricultural production was displayed in the material and physical wealth of the city. The champions of the consumer-city model tend to minimalise the importance of trade and exchange. It is true that the Roman city did not mass-produce goods on a large scale for export to specific markets. Production, where it did occur, particularly in the urban context, was on a small scale and centred upon the workshop rather than the manufactory or factory. This small-scale production is dismissed as unimportant, because the exponents of the consumer-city model tend to define trade as the production of goods on a large scale for export (Jongman 1988). The academic emphasis on the city as the consumer of wealth from its rural hinterland has marginalised the small-scale production in the city, which served the needs of the surrounding rural population (for the alternative of a 'service city' see Engels 1990, in particular 121–42). The macro scale of analysis taken by the exponents of the consumer-city model obscures many important features of Roman cities and, in particular, many of those which are strongly attested in Pompeii, where there were a number of small-scale workshops that produced finished goods for sale to others in the city (La Torre 1988 surveys these; see earlier Mustilli 1950). Some of these products were traded over considerable distances. For example, the ceramic assemblage known as 'Pompeian Red Ware' (produced in Campania) has a wide distribution in the western empire (Peacock 1977). The scale of trade and exchange involved in the creation

51

of this distribution was not necessarily all that large. However, it remains the case that goods produced in Pompeii were traded over considerable distances, even though the producers of these goods need not have been directly involved in any form of production for export.

The nature of trade can be illustrated by a find of a box of imported lamps and bowls to Pompeii. In the *tablinum* of an *atrium* house (8.5.9) a wooden box was found which contained seventy-six *terra sigillata* bowls and thirty-seven lamps. The *terra sigillata* bowls were of south Gaulish origin. Fifty-four of the bowls were of form 37 and twenty-three corresponded to form 29. The thirty-seven lamps displayed a similar uniformity and were stamped with *fortis* and *communis*, which suggests that they were of a north Italian origin. Neither the bowls nor the lamps showed any sign of use. In fact, it seems likely that they had been delivered shortly prior to the eruption of Vesuvius in AD 79 (Atkinson 1914). The uniformity of the bowls and lamps suggests that they were not for domestic consumption in 8.5.9. Instead, it seems likely that they were destined for some form of trade, exchange or distribution by the occupants of the house. This box of bowls and lamps epitomises the small scale of trade (contra Harris 1980). The *terra sigillata* bowls had their origins in southern Gaul, but the lamps were from northern Italy. At some point between these points of origin and Pompeii, they were placed together in the box for delivery to 8.5.9. It appears strange that *terra sigillata* should be brought from Gaul to Pompeii when there was a source of this product on the Bay of Naples (Pucci 1981). Significantly, the majority of *terra sigillata* found at Pompeii was produced near Puteoli (Pucci 1977). Equally, to export lamps from northern Italy to Pompeii does not conform to the notions of economic rationality that underlie our models of ancient trade (Harris 1980: 134). Lamps were produced locally in Pompeii, for example at 1.20.2–3 (Cerulli Irelli 1977; De Caro 1974). The imported products that found their way to Pompeii would have been subject to transport costs that local products would not have incurred. However, it would appear time and again, as we shall see, that an imported product could compete directly with a product of local origin. Such a situation contradicts the economic rationality underlying the consumer-city model. It would appear that there were a large number of small consignments of products, such as that found at 8.5.9, being traded or exchanged around the Mediterranean. The total production and consumption of these small consignments of goods formed an important part of the urban economy of Pompeii (for the scale of use of lamps for domestic lighting see Castiglione Morelli 1983).

However, before we begin to analyse the local patterns of production and consumption in Pompeii, we must set the city of Pompeii in a wider economic perspective. Geographically, Pompeii was the *entrepôt* for the Sarno river valley (Strabo 247C = 5.4.8). It had good river connections with the towns of this economic hinterland. Also, it formed part of an economy based upon the luxury villas of the Bay of Naples and the wider Campanian economy, which was centred upon Puteoli (D'Arms 1970: 116–67). In fact, Frederiksen has argued that the towns of Campania, including Capua, Cumae, Neapolis, Pompeii and Puteoli, form a single socio-economic unit (Frederiksen 1984: 321). This socio-economic unit was not solely concerned with consumption of produce imported into the port of Puteoli (Frederiksen 1980/1). In fact, he goes on to suggest that the agricultural hinterland of Campania provided Puteoli with a wealth of produce that complemented its function as the port of Rome (Frederiksen 1984: 325). Pompeii's close proximity to Puteoli in economic terms meant that its pattern of trade with other parts of the empire mirrors that of Puteoli.

Pottery can be used as an index to establish the pattern, though not necessarily the scale, of trade between regions (Greene 1992 provides an introduction to pottery studies). Pottery, as such, was not normally the major product traded. It tended to be traded alongside other more important goods (Peacock 1982: 154). Pottery manufactured in the Pompeian region has a distinctive red clay, which has been petrologically identified by volcanic elements from the region (Peacock 1977: 147). Equally, rigorous analysis has established the places for production throughout the empire of many types of pottery and, in particular, *terra sigillata* and *amphorae*. This evidence can be used to define the trading links of Pompeii and provide a wider context for production and consumption patterns in the city.

Products that were imported into Pompeii came from a variety of regions. Pucci's study of over 1,600 *terra sigillata* bowls provides a guide to the areas from which goods were brought to Pompeii (Pucci 1977): 29 per cent of the bowls were of Campanian origin, 35 per cent were produced in Italy, 23 per cent were manufactured in the eastern Mediterranean, 12 per cent came from southern Gaul and an insignificant number were of African origin. These figures provide illuminating detail about the nature of trade to Pompeii. Even though Puteoli was a centre for *terra sigillata* production, it does not dominate the assemblage found at Pompeii. There are a significant number of vessels produced outside of the immediate locality. As Pucci argues, the importance of the East should not be underestimated. The material from southern Gaul may comprise 12 per cent of the total assemblage, but almost 50 per cent of the south Gaulish products comes from the single box found at 8.5.9. Therefore, from this pottery assemblage, we can see that Pompeii had strong trading contact with the eastern Mediterranean as well as locally with Puteoli and other regions of Italy (see Slane 1989 for a Corinthian perspective). Such a pattern is mirrored in the assemblages of *amphorae* from Pompeii.[1] Panella has forcefully argued in her study of *amphorae* that those bearing Greek *tituli* are also of a shape that is associated with wine production in the Aegean (Panella 1974/5; Panella and Fano 1974/5; Tchernia 1986: 240–1). The prominence of these *amphorae* in the assemblages from Pompeii suggests a strong link with this area of the Mediterranean. The nature and scale of trade are revealed in the *tituli* found on *amphorae* in Pompeii. If these *amphorae* had been traded in bulk, we could expect them to have uniform *tituli*. However, the recorded *tituli* in *CIL* IV on amphorae found at the same location in Pompeii seldom have the same format, which suggests that they were traded in small lots to individual buyers (Mouritsen 1988: 16–17; for an Aegean perspective on this trade pattern see Slane 1989). Again the scale of trade should not be seen as production for export, but as production that was exported.

Pottery studies can also provide an indication of the nature of exports from Pompeii. Pompeian Red Ware has been found at a number of locations. It should be noted that any pattern of pottery distribution is dependent upon the number of modern pottery studies. The intensity with which pottery has been studied varies enormously. It has been most strongly studied in northern Europe and least studied in the eastern Mediterranean: therefore, we only see part of the picture at present. Pompeian Red Ware fabric 1 has been found in Greece, north Africa, Italy, Germany and Britain (Peacock 1977). Therefore it has a fairly wide distribution, and further study may show that it probably had a very similar distribution pattern to *terra sigillata* produced in the vicinity of Puteoli (Pucci 1981). Pompeii, like Puteoli, was closely linked to Rome. One of the major products that was produced for the market at Rome was wine. This can be demonstrated with reference to stratified finds of *amphorae* from Ostia: the distinctive Vesuvian clays identify a group of vessels with the region of the Sarno river valley and the Sorrentine peninsula. The find of 180 *amphorae* associated with *terra sigillata* provided an early Augustan date for the total assemblage. This assemblage provides us with a representative sample of the maritime wine trade to Rome. The largest single group of *amphorae* were those of Pompeian or Sorrentine origin, which represented 28 per cent of the total assemblage (figures from Tchernia 1986: 153–4). This figure was rivalled only by north Italian *amphorae*, representing 23 per cent of the total assemblage. Thus, the destination for many products from Campania was the metropolis of Rome. As Jongman has so ably pointed out, the city of Pompeii did not produce manufactured goods specifically for export (Jongman 1988): there was neither a mass market nor the mass production of goods. However, goods were traded and exchanged for other products from other regions of the Mediterranean (maritime trade: D'Arms and Kopff 1980; D'Arms 1981; Rickman 1980; Garnsey 1988; Panella 1981). The scale of production was small, but there were a large number of products produced. This suggests that the producers were not a dominant element in the economy of the city, but their production was a social necessity for the city to function. It was the *negotiatores* (traders) who facilitated trade, by bringing goods from one location and selling them in another. The producers themselves seldom came into contact with the consumer at a distance. However, they sold products in the city to visiting traders in small lots.

Secondary products, such as pottery, were traded in shipments of primary products, such as wine or oil, that had been produced to be exported. The pattern of trade indicated by pottery distribution does not follow the lines predicted by modern economics. In many cases, an imported product could compete with a locally produced product of a similar nature (see Peacock 1982: 12–52 for an ethnographic study of pottery production in the Mediterranean in the twentieth century). This is indicative of the complexity of trade in the Roman Mediterranean.

The urban economy was primarily based upon small-scale workshop production (see Andreau 1974 and Jongman 1988: 212–25 on the scale of finance). The workshop is a unit of production associated normally with a single specialised product. In pre-industrial cities, there tends to be speciali-sation in products rather than in the processes of production (Sjoberg 1960: 197). The form of production in the workshop differs from household production: the workshop is concerned with production on a full-time basis throughout the year, whereas household production tends to be a part-time activity supplementing other economic activities (Peacock 1982: 6–11, 25–41). The workshop, typically, produces a product using specialised equipment, which need not be widely available. Such specialised equipment appears in the archaeological record from Pompeii. The fact that this equip-ment is of a specialised nature allows for the identification of baking, metal production and cloth production. Significantly, the equipment involved does not tend to appear in domestic contexts. Thus, various forms of workshop define the place of production in Pompeii. Also, the fact that production took place in workshops rather than any domestic context suggests that the producers formed a distinct group in the city. However, it should be noted that many workshops were located in converted *atrium*-style houses. Some groups of craftsmen appear in electoral graffiti (for example, goldsmiths: *CIL* 4.710). However, the absence of, for example, goldsmiths from the archaeological record is striking. In other cases, it is difficult to match up archaeologically defined workshops with craftsmen attested in the graffiti (Jongman 1988: 159–84, compare La Torre 1988). However, the operators of workshops did form a number of distinctive groups within the city, and we might expect certain streets or areas of the city to be associated with certain types of production. Therefore, in what follows, the position of archaeologically distinct workshops will be exam-ined to evaluate the position of workshop manufacturing in Pompeii.

Bakeries can be identified by the presence of mills for grinding corn into flour or by the presence of a large oven (Mayeske 1972). The distribution of bakeries in Pompeii is uneven: there are few in the excavated areas to the east of the city, and few in close proximity to the forum. However, there is a strong concentration of bakeries along Via di Stabia and also towards the north of the city. This might suggest that this general trend in the location of bakeries reflects the hinterland from where the grain was brought to the city

Plate 4.1 Bakery: mill and oven

(i.e. from the area to the north of the city). The only known *horrea* are located near the forum and underneath Casa del Marinaio in Vicolo dei Soprastanti (Franklin 1990). These would have been convenient for grain brought in from the North.

Those bakeries that do not have mills, and therefore did not grind their own flour, are concentrated in the central area. These bakeries only baked bread or other products in their ovens for sale on the premises. This type of bakery is found mostly in *Regio 7* to the east of the forum. Indeed, it is in this area that we find the highest concentration of bakeries. In Via degli Augustali there are a total of seven bakeries. This would suggest that this street would have been associated with bread production and retailing by the inhabitants of Pompeii. In contrast, those bakeries without facilities for retailing were located away from the main through-routes of the city. This would facilitate deliveries of grain, without congesting a busy street. Also, bakeries that ground their own flour required a relatively large area for the mills. For example, bakeries with mills are sometimes found in converted *atrium* houses and the mills are located in the peristyle. Therefore, those bakeries involved in the grinding of flour and production tended to be located in areas away from the through-routes of the city, where space was available for the location of mills. It should be noted that the mills were specialised equipment. These mills have been petrologically studied to establish the provenance of the stone: Peacock has successfully located the rock as predominantly Umbrian and has identified the quarry close to Orvieto (Peacock 1980; 1986; 1989; Williams-Thorpe 1988). The mills were transported over a considerable distance from Orvieto to Pompeii. It would seem likely that the mills from Orvieto were initially transported to Rome, where they were sold on to Pompeian buyers. It would appear from Peacock's series of studies of Pompeian mills that the Orvieto-quarried mills supplanted locally quarried mills (Peacock 1989). Therefore, the imported mills successfully competed with mills quarried in the vicinity of Pompeii. The mill trade provides us with an example of a bulky material being traded over considerable distances and competing with a local product of a similar nature.

The archaeological definition of a bakery by the presence of a mill or oven does not account for the total distribution and sale of bread and other bakery products in Pompeii. Bread could be sold from other shops and stalls at other locations in the city. The data for such locations do not appear in the archaeological record. However, the distribution pattern of bakeries does suggest that bakery production in Pompeii was concentrated on the through-routes to the north of the city and in the central area to the east of the forum, with a strong concentration of bakeries in Via degli Augustali.

Moeller identified a number of archaeologically distinct workshops in his study of textile manufacture at Pompeii (Moeller 1976). Unfortunately, the available evidence for finds of loom weights is negligible (Moeller 1976: 39–41 mentions a total of fifty loom weights from a single location in his

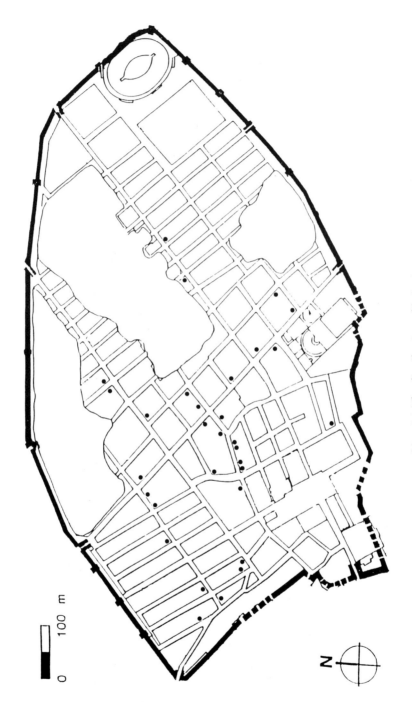

Map 4.1 The distribution of bakeries

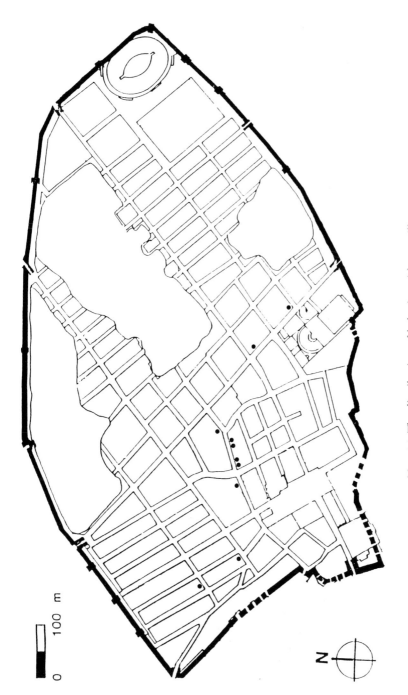

Map 4.2 The distribution of bakeries without mills

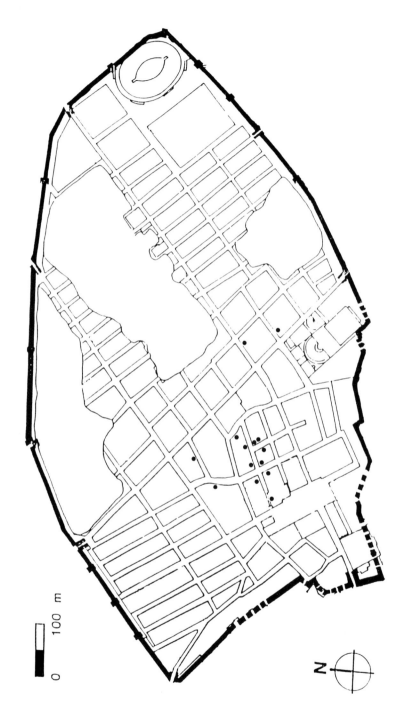

Map 4.3 The distribution of *officinae lanifricariae*

discussion of weaving. Jongman 1988 does not supplement this evidence). However, Moeller did identify a number of workshops in the archaeological record with processes associated with wool and cloth cleaning. He supplemented this archaeological evidence with graffiti that mentioned fullers, dyers, felters and cleaners. In doing so, he attempted to link the position of the graffiti with neighbouring workshops. Such a methodology has proved to be unsound, because electoral graffiti were seldom placed in the vicinity of the place of residence or work of those mentioned in the graffiti (Mouritsen 1988: 18–27). Further, Moeller interpreted the evidence for wool production in Pompeii in terms of production for export. He suggested that this process of production was controlled by the *collegium* of the fullers. In his interpretation of the Pompeian evidence, Moeller overemphasised the scale of production. Jongman has thoroughly demonstrated that all of Moeller's conclusions about textile production were fundamentally flawed (Jongman 1988: 155–86), but in doing so, Jongman tends to minimalise the importance of Moeller's original fieldwork in Pompeii. What Moeller did succeed in doing was to define a number of archaeologically distinct workshops (Jongman 1988: 168–9 admits this). What Moeller ascribes as *officinae lanifricariae* are workshops that include vats and furnaces (Moeller 1976: 30–5); his *officinae tinctoriae* also feature vats and furnaces (Moeller 1976: 35–9). His *fullonicae* are defined by the presence of vats and treading stools (Moeller 1976: 41–51). It is the specialised equipment of these workshops that allows for their definition.[2] Jongman concluded that textile production in Pompeii was for local consumption, because, in comparison to the textile industries of early modern Europe, production in Pompeii was on a much smaller economic scale (Jongman 1988: 184–6). We need not concern ourselves with the economics of production here: our concern is with the spatial dimensions of production in the city. Were these archaeologically distinct workshops concentrated in particular areas? The *officinae lanifricariae* were concentrated in *Regio 7* to the east of the forum. The majority of these workshops were located in or close to Vicolo del Balcone Pensile. Other *officinae lanifricariae* were located in Via dell'Abbondanza and Vicolo del Menandro. In contrast, the *fullonicae* were not concentrated in *Regio 7*, but were distributed throughout the city. However, their distribution was not even, with a slight concentration towards the Porta del Vesuvio. Other *fullonicae* were located in Via di Mercurio, Via di Nola, Via degli Augustali, Via dell'Abbondanza and Vicolo del Menandro. There would appear to have been a tendency for *fullonicae* to have been located upon the through-routes of the city. The *officinae tinctoriae* have a similar pattern of distribution to that of the *fullonicae*. These workshops occur on Via di Stabia, Via di Nola, Via dell'Abbondanza and in Vicolo degli Scheletri and Vicolo dell'Efebro. It is most noticeable that these three types of workshop were seldom located in *Regiones* 6 and 8 and, where they were located in *Regio* 1, there was a tendency for these workshops to have been located close

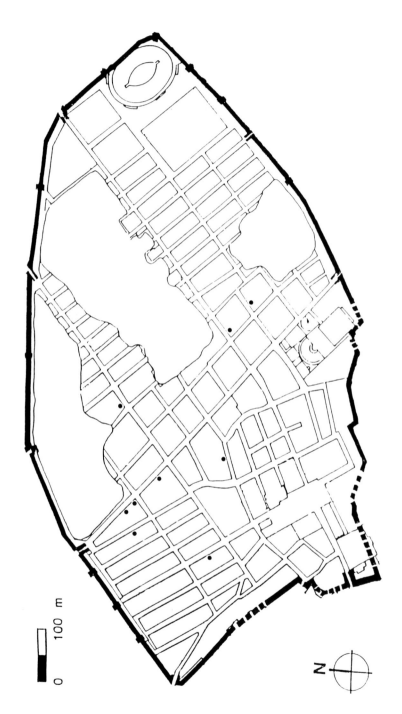

100 m

0

Map 4.4 The distribution of *fullonicae*

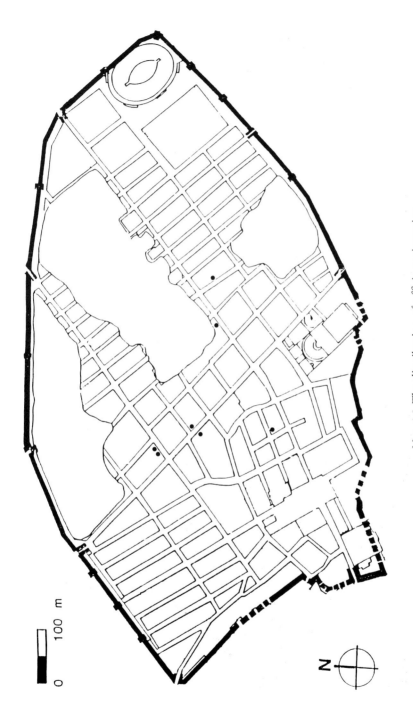

Map 4.5 The distribution of *officinae tinctoriae*

to through-routes and towards the centre of the city, rather than more isolated areas to the east of the city. This might suggest that these workshops were located in areas that were not dominated by the residential requirements of the inhabitants.

Workshops associated with metalworking can also be defined archaeologically. Gralfs (1988), in her study of metalworking in Pompeii, has six criteria for the definition of a metal workshop. These include: specialised tools, equipment, worked material, moulds and casts, worked clay, and inscriptions and shopsigns (Gralfs 1988: 11). From these criteria, she has identified thirteen locations for metalworking in the city (Gralfs 1988: 12–70). Most of these workshops were located upon the through-routes of the city, and do not appear to have been concentrated in any one area. However, we do find workshops grouped closely together. There appears to have been a total absence of metalworking from the central area to the east of the forum and in *Regio* 8. Like the textile-producing workshops, the metal workshops avoided the residential areas associated with *Regiones* 1, 5, 6 and 8. Their location upon through-routes may reflect the need to transport raw materials to the workshop from outside the city, which is also reflected in the location of a workshop outside Porta del Vesuvio. This might explain why metalworking is not found in the central areas of the city associated with *Regiones* 7 and 9.

Pompeii was noted for its production of fine-quality *garum* (fish sauce) by Pliny (*N.H.* 31.94). To date, excavations have located a single *garum* shop at 1.12.8, which, as Curtis points out, was not a centre of production (Curtis 1979; see also his other articles upon *garum* from Pompeii, 1983, 1984a, 1984b, 1985 and 1991 summarising earlier work). It would appear that the production of *garum* did not occur within the city walls. The most likely location for this production would have been at Pompeii's port facility on the river Sarno. However, although Pompeii was a renowned centre for *garum* production, *garum* and other fish-sauce products were imported to the city (Manacorda 1977). It would appear that *garum* imported from Spain could compete with locally produced *garum*. This would appear to be one of the many economic contradictions associated with the ancient world: Pompeii produced, exported and imported *garum*. Curtis estimates from the *tituli* of *amphorae* found at Pompeii that 71 per cent were locally produced. It could be argued that *garum* varied in quality and was destined for different social groups accordingly (Curtis 1985: 215). However, any examination of the find spots of *amphorae* with *tituli* in Pompeii, published in *CIL* 4, suggests that *garum* was widely available to the population, from the rich to the customers at the *popinae*.

Finally, we need to discuss the significance of agricultural production in the city. Jashemski's work was pioneering in the study of environmental data at the site. Her work concentrated upon excavating and, in many cases re-excavating, agricultural plots in *Regiones* 1 and 2 to the south-east of the

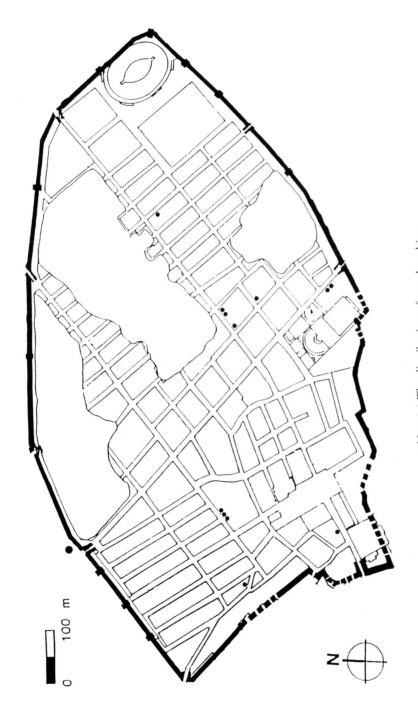

Map 4.6 The distribution of metalworking

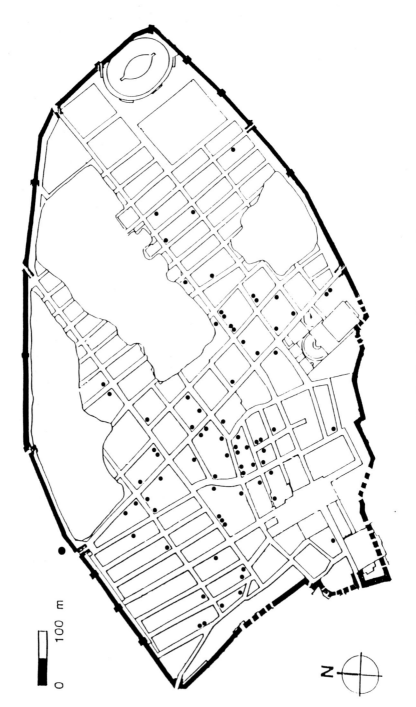

Map 4.7 The distribution of all known workshops

city (for a full account see Jashemski 1979). Excavation and conservation in this area have continued in the 1980s and 1990s funded by FIO (see recent reports in *Rivista di Studi Pompeiane*). Jashemski's excavations identified a number of large agricultural plots within the circuit of the city walls. In a large plot (1.5) opposite the amphitheatre, she identified 1,423 vine roots and evidence that olives were cultivated here (Jashemski 1979: 203). Clearly, wine was produced here and sold at a shop on Via dell'Abbondanza. There was also a small *triclinium* set up to serve visitors to the games at the amphitheatre (Jashemski 1979: 215). Other vineyards were identified at 1.20.1, 1.20.5, 3.7, 9.9.6–7 (Jashemski 1979: 228–32). A market garden was identified in the southern part of *Insula* 1.15. Greene (1986: 97) has argued that this garden produced far in excess of the needs for consumption at this location and that produce was sold elsewhere in the city. Produce included grapes, olives, nuts, fruit and vegetables. Jashemski observed that a similar planting pattern occurred in other parts of the city excavated in the nineteenth century (Jashemski 1979: 236: these include 6.6.1 and 9.1.20). She also identified an orchard at 1.22 and a number of sites associated with market gardening (Jashemski 1979: 243–50: 1.21.2–3; 251–65: 7.11.1, 7.10.14, 2.8.6; 171: 7.11.11/14; 188–90: 1.20.5). She argued that these locations could have utilised the Campanian soil and climate to grow at least three different crops each year (Jashemski 1979: 287). The location of these agricultural plots was predominantly in the south-eastern part of the city near the amphitheatre. This reflects not only the area in which Jashemski did most of her work, but also that in this area there appears to have been a lower density of settlement and hence less pressure on space for residential purposes. Also the *insulae* in this area are mostly sited upon a south-facing slope, an agricultural advantage which other parts of the city did not have (Colum. 3.2.6). However, market gardening was also conducted in the more densely populated areas of the city, including *Regio* 7 to the east of the forum (at 7.11.1, 7.10.14 and 7.11.11/14). This would suggest that the division between town and country was not as pronounced as we tend to expect.[3] The soil in Pompeii was so productive that pressure to convert areas of the city from agricultural use into housing was resisted. Animal husbandry has been neglected in the study of Pompeii; but it was practised inside the city walls. For example, two skeletons of cows were found during the excavation of the Casa del Fauno (Jashemski 1979: 216; *NS* 1900: 31). Therefore, to date, we have only a partial picture of agricultural production in Pompeii (on market gardening at Rome see Carandini 1988: 339–57). However, productive gardens account for 9.7 per cent of the urban area, while ornamental gardens account for 5.4 per cent (figures from Jashemski 1979: 24). Thus, agricultural production was an important feature in the urban landscape of Pompeii. Produce from these agricultural plots would have been for local consumption, rather than export to other cities and regions.

It would appear that the pattern of productive land use in Pompeii was not organised according to function. We do not find areas exclusively associated with craft workshops or productive gardens. The land use of the city was a mixture of functional categories: the residential areas were not separated from areas of retailing or production. Such a pattern of land use is similar to patterns established in the Adobe city at Mendoza in Argentina (Morris 1987). Morris' account of these is instructive for understanding land-use patterns in Pompeii. Virtually all of Mendoza was destroyed in 1861 by seismic activity. The city was rebuilt with buildings of two or three storeys, because the inhabitants feared the collapse of tall buildings during future earthquakes. The pattern of development in individual blocks is similar to that at Pompeii, because 'each house sought a street frontage and no alleys were made dividing the blocks, so that houses occupied the block periphery leaving a hollow centre' (Morris 1987: 66; for a similar process in Pompeii, see Ling 1983 on *Insula* 1.10). Morris notes that the pattern of land use appears to lack logic, with housing mixed in with retailing, workshops, car-repair yards and wholesale establishments. To account for this disordered land-use pattern, so familiar to the Pompeianist, Morris (1987: 69–71) identifies a number of significant factors. First of all, a total lack of planning controls or zoning has prevented the creation of social or economic divisions in space. These would have caused certain locations to have been preferable for the location of certain enterprises. Secondly, the uniform chessboard colonial urban layout of houses and streets causes few points or lines to concentrate activity or intensify land use. Thirdly, in the absence of municipal controls upon land use, the owners of individual properties have complete jurisdiction over land use. This has resulted in the subdivision of property, which causes any developer to have to deal with a multiplicity of owners in the development of a single block. Finally, the low-density land-use pattern of the Adobe city in Mendoza, in itself, allows for a mixture of land uses, because the land is of high value, but the structures on it are of low value (Morris 1987: 70–1). The high value of the land in combination with a multiplicity of owners prevents the development of high rise tenements in this zone of Mendoza. Therefore, in Mendoza, the combination of a street grid, low-density land use and a lack of municipal planning results in a diverse land-use pattern similar to that of Pompeii. Significantly, the conditions for urban development in Mendoza and Pompeii were identical. Thus, it should come as no surprise that, in Pompeii, we find a diverse pattern of land use, which includes units of agricultural production and small-scale workshops.

In terms of production and consumption, the city of Pompeii produced materials for sale within the city, as well as being the recipient of goods from its agricultural hinterland. Some of the products from Pompeii and its rural hinterland were exported from the city region. At the same time, products were imported into the city by sea from other areas of the Mediterranean, many of which competed with local products, from the city and its hinterland. This economic reality is difficult to comprehend in the context of the consumer-city model, in which products, incurring transport costs, should not be able to compete with local products of a similar type (Jongman 1988: 138–41). It might be possible to explain this evidence away as an anomaly produced by the economic disruption caused by the earthquake of AD 62 (Andreau 1973). However, the AD 62 earthquake does provide an easy solution to any aspect of Pompeii that does not conform to our expectations of Roman towns. Alternatively, we might see these imports not in terms of trade at all. The movement of goods such as wine or *garum* may represent not trade but the concentration of a person's movable wealth, derived from their ownership of property in the provinces, to Italy. If these items are seen as representing trade, an alternative model can explain their presence at Pompeii: it can be argued that the imported goods to Pompeii were brought to the site along with more valuable cargoes. These cargoes would have contained products not available in Campania which could incur large transport costs without making them uncompetitive. The more valuable cargoes would incur the transport costs of the whole shipment, and that part of the cargo associated with, for example, *garum* would have been priced without the addition of transport costs. In consequence, such products could have competed directly with locally produced *garum*. Therefore, in effect, the maritime trade in staples rode upon the back of a trade in luxury items (see Wallace-Hadrill 1990 on the spread of luxury). This situation would have produced the mixed assemblage of imported and locally produced ceramics. Equally, the demand and size of the mass market for wine at Rome allowed for the export of wine and other products from the Pompeian region. This is an important amendment to the consumer-city model set out by Jongman (1988) for Pompeii. Therefore, the urban economy of Pompeii does not conform exactly to the consumer-city model. However, as Carandini has found, the correspondence between the Roman city and Weber's ideal types of the consumer and producer city is not an exact fit when the evidence for production and consumption is considered (Carandini 1988: 337–8). The Roman city was more diverse than these ideal types suggest, and was neither a consumer nor a producer city. However, goods were produced and consumed. Between producer and consumer there was a network of traders that only leaves a record of itself in the ceramic assemblages available to the archaeologist, which have at best given us an indication of the complex patterns of trade and exchange to and from Pompeii. The economic complexity of this trade and exchange should not be underestimated. Products manufactured in the many workshops of Pompeii competed with imported products from other areas. The workshops at Pompeii did manufacture goods that were exported; this export was not conducted with specific markets in mind, but it is more than likely that, initially, these products were exchanged in the markets of Puteoli, the port of Rome, from where they were taken to the markets of the capital. Traders in Rome and Puteoli would have diffused goods produced in Pompeii throughout the empire.

5

DEVIANT BEHAVIOUR

In this chapter, Pompeii is examined to identify the areas in which deviant behaviour was tolerated, and those in which it was restricted. Deviant behaviour can be defined as behaviour that is condemned by a substantial proportion of the population, but is not considered to be beyond the limits of toleration by many people (Cohen 1980: 1). Deviant behaviour is delineated and created by those social groups that label this behaviour as abnormal (Becker 1987: 8; Rubington and Wennberg 1987). In effect, the deviants in a society are those people who contravene the rules of that society (Goodie 1984: 3). Typically, deviant behaviour includes prostitution, 'excessive' alcoholic consumption and gambling. In the Roman Empire deviants were defined legally and termed *infames*. They were sharply defined by reason of numerous forms of wrongful or unseemly conduct, and were subjected to serious disabilities (see, e.g., *CIL* 1.593; Garnsey 1970: 185–91). The group included shameful trades: those of the prostitute, the brothel owner, actors, gladiators and the trainers of gladiators. Legally, the *infames* could neither act for someone else nor appoint someone to act for them (Buckland 1921: 92–3). However, the control of deviancy would not have been limited to its legal definition. It seems likely that deviant behaviour was policed or, at least, regulated by the aediles (Robinson 1991: 138; see Gell. 4.15 for specific examples and Nippel 1984 on policing at Rome). This would have caused deviant behaviour to have been located in areas of the city that would have been tolerant of it.

The literary evidence of Latin authors provides a context for the definition and location of deviant behaviour and deviants. In literature, the location of deviance was in the brothels and *popinae* of the city, whose customers were the slaves, gladiators, drunks, thieves, gamblers, undertakers and bargemen (Hor., *Ep.* 1.14.22; Mart. 9.32; Sen., *Contr.* 1.2.10; Plaut., *Trin.* 1021; Juv. 8.171; Amm.Marc. 14.6.25; for discussion see Kampen 1981). In effect, this literary stereotype sees the location of the *infames* and their provision of services as suitable only for the undesirables in society. However, the reality might be rather different. The provision of services by the *infames* may have been a necessary feature of the structure of Roman society. Therefore, in what follows, the locations of prostitution, public drinking and gambling in Pompeii will be examined with reference to the literary and archaeological evidence to establish in which areas of Pompeii deviant behaviour was tolerated or restricted.

The prostitute was seen as the opposite of the Roman matron. The prostitute was easily distinguished by her short brightly coloured dress, elaborate hairstyle and make-up (Gardner 1986: 251). However, the prostitute should not be seen as the antithesis or enemy of the family and family values but, instead, as the preserver of those values (Goodie 1984: 151). Horace reported the remarks of Cato, when he met two young men coming out of a brothel. Cato commended their action in coming to the brothel rather than becoming involved in an adulterous affair with another man's wife (Hor., *Sat.* 1.2.30–7, 1.2.119–34). The possibility of an affair with an unmarried woman is not considered, because most women married for the first time at an early age (Rousselle 1992: 303–7; Saller and Shaw 1984; Shaw 1987, 1991). In contrast, men tended to marry later, in their twenties (Saller 1987). This imbalance in the age of marriage of male and female may have caused the prostitute to be a necessity for the maintenance of a society based upon monogamous marriage. Furthermore, as Rousselle (1992) points out, the purpose of marriage was reproduction rather than sexual love (see also Dixon 1992: 62–3). She stresses that sexual love between husband and wife was a disaster for the woman, because she would die from repeated child bearing. Rousselle sees it as equally disastrous for the husband not to find a sexual partner outside of marriage, because again the wife would die from repeated child bearing (Rousselle 1992: 301–27). The need for the husband to have a sexual partner outside of marriage was problematic, because the availability of such partners was limited by the norms of society. For husbands, adultery with a married woman, if discovered, would bring harsh penalties under the Augustan legislation against adultery (Gardner 1986: 127–31 provides a summary of the legal position; see Cohen 1991). An alternative could have been for the husband to have a sexual relationship with a slave in their household (Foucault 1984b: 73–80 points to this distinction). However, this might disrupt the structure of power relations in that household (Corbin 1990: 4–9). One alternative, for the husband, was to visit a prostitute. The recognition of this need was reflected in Roman law: the husband's sexual activity with a prostitute was not recognised as a form of adultery. The adultery law was promulgated to promote the stability of marriage and the family. For that family to be stable, it would have been necessary to ensure the possibility of the wife/mother surviving. In any case, sex with a prostitute did not endanger the marriage or family structure of inheritance. In fact, prostitution promoted the stability of the family in Rome's patriarchal society.

However, the prostitute, as the total opposite of the Roman matron, was perceived as a threat to the majority in the Roman city, because she was a woman who did not fulfil the Roman ideal of womanhood. Thus, it was necessary for the prostitutes of the city to be regulated and controlled (cf. nineteenth-century Paris, Corbin 1990). Those deriving their income solely from prostitution had to present themselves to the aediles of the city to be registered (Tac., *Ann.* 2.85; Suet., *Tib.* 35; Dig. 25.7.1.2, 48.5.11.(10).2; Paul., *Sent.* 2.26.11). This would allow the aediles to know who was and who was not a prostitute. We may assume that there was a penalty for non-registration. Presumably, registration included the place of residence or work of the prostitute. Women workers in bars or *popinae* were considered to have been prostitutes, but did not need to be registered, because their income was not exclusively derived from prostitution (Gardner 1986: 251 citing Dig. 23.2.43). The prostitute, pimp or brothel owner was taxed at the rate of a single sexual act (Suet., *Gaius* 40. Prices in Pompeii vary from 2 to 16 *asses*: Duncan-Jones 1982: 246). This process of registration and taxation of prostitutes gave the aediles a powerful body of knowledge about prostitution in the city (Foucault 1977). How the aediles used this information is uncertain. Gardner (1986: 251) suggests that the aedile would have visited the brothels of the city as part of his duties. However, there might have been more to this process of registration than just finding out who was a prostitute. In any case, the prostitute was distinguished from other women by her dress and gesture. The point of registration of prostitutes may have been to control their activities and limit their activities to areas of the city in which the population would have been more tolerant of deviant behaviour.[1] Ideally, patriarchal societies make prostitution invisible to women, children and the elderly, and it is young males who are normally more tolerant of the presence of prostitution in their neighbourhood (Cohen 1980: 5). If such a situation was the case in the Roman city, we would expect to find the prostitute located in certain marginal areas of the city, away from those areas where they might come into contact with women and children of respectable families of the elite.

The mechanics of getting a customer to the brothel in the literary sources are significant in the context of the spatial distribution of prostitution. These methods appear as a subtle part of a plot in the *Satyricon* by Petronius: a man visiting Puteoli could not find his way back to the inn he was staying at (see Ling 1990 on the problems of strangers finding their way around Pompeii), so he asked an old woman selling vegetables from the country, where he lived; she answered that she did know and took him to a rather obscure part of the city, and then told him his home was behind a curtain that led into a brothel. The man's friend, Ascyltos, had also become lost and had asked a *paterfamilias* the way. The *paterfamilias* took him to the same brothel not because he thought he was a customer, but because the *paterfamilias* had taken him to be a prostitute (Petr., *Sat.* 7–9). The important part of the story seems to be that the part of the city where the brothel was located was rather obscure.

At Rome, the location of prostitution was used by Martial to typify the Subura, which according to our literary evidence was an area of Rome that contained only a few aristocratic houses and was one of the areas within Rome that was associated with people of lower status and many forms of deviant behaviour (Mart., *Ep.* 6.66, 11.61, 11.71). What is more, it was an area into which children of the elite would not venture. For the male youth, who had undergone the Roman rite of passage from childhood to manhood, the Subura offered a new-found fascination (Pers., *Sat.* 5.30–40). An informal part of this rite of passage may have included the sexual initiation of the sons of the elite with prostitutes in the Subura. Significantly, prostitution was invisible to the children of the elite and was seen only by adult members of this group. Other locations of prostitution were in the vicinity of public buildings of entertainment, such as the circus, the theatre, the stadium and the baths (S.H.A., *Elagab.* 26.3). Whether these buildings were being used for their main functional purpose at the time is uncertain. The public buildings not in use after dark would have been ideal spots for prostitution, because there were no inhabitants whose moral sensibilities could be outraged (Cohen 1980: 5). The baths were also a most suitable place for prostitutes to work from, for they would have been in contact with a high proportion of the male population (Foucault 1984a: 251–2). Martial also points out that the tombs and the walls were locations for prostitutes to work from (Mart., *Ep.* 1.34, 3.82; Gardner 1986: 251–2). These examples demonstrate that the prostitute was most prominent in those areas of the city that were isolated from other activities and, in particular, other women and children not involved in prostitution.

The location of the prostitute in the literary conception of the city was in the narrow alleyways, amongst the tombs, in the shelter of empty public buildings and under the walls of the city. All of these places were isolated from passing observers, but their position would have been known to customers of the prostitutes and the city population generally. It is an important point that the city population would not have come into contact with prostitution unless they actively sought it out.

Evidence for buildings exclusively designed for the sale of sex has frequently been noted in the archaeological record of Pompeii. The number of brothels in Pompeii used to be as high as about thirty-five or more. However, at present, a certain amount of re-evaluation of the evidence is in progress, and the most recent assessment suggests there are in fact only nine purpose-built brothel sites, seven of which are single *cellae* (Wallace-Hadrill 1994). Their location is concentrated in the central area of the city to the east of the forum. There are also two more sites in *Regio* 9. The brothels are sited in streets that are not through-routes and were isolated from the main areas of social activity. Also, they are located in streets in which there are very few main entrances into large *atrium* houses. This might suggest that the brothels were deliberately located out of the view of the elite.

Plate 5.1 The large brothel at 7.12.18

However, the brothels in most cases tend to adjoin large *atrium* houses, and most of the *cellae* were located in premises that were architecturally part of an *atrium* house. For example, 7.13.4 has two *cellae* located at the rear of the house next to its door in Vicolo degli Scheletri (Eschebach 1982, compare *Insula* 7.12; Nishida and Hori 1992). There is also another *cella* further down this street. At some point, the single cell associated with prostitution was divided off from the main house. What the relationship was between the owner of this large house and the prostitutes using these two *cellae* remains in question. At the front of this house, we find a perfectly respectable *fauces*, leading into an *atrium*. However, at the back of the house, the entrance is next door to two *cellae*, which had been constructed for prostitution. This seems to highlight the fact that the public face of the household was to be viewed from the *fauces*, rather than the door at the rear. Ideally, the *fauces* was located upon a main thoroughfare, rather than down an alley. Hence, on the main thoroughfares of the city we find the entrances of *atrium*-type houses competing for space with shops, bars, etc. It would have been particularly difficult for people outside the household to identify the other entrances, apart from the *fauces*, into an *atrium* house. Hence, in the example of 7.13.4, a stranger would not associate the doorway next to the *cellae* with the rather imposing *atrium* house they had seen in Via dell'Abbondanza. However, the person seeking the prostitute might note a series of phalluses on the road and walls of this *insula*, which would have guided that person from the wide thoroughfare of Via dell'Abbondanza, up Vicolo di Eumachia and into Vicolo degli Scheletri to the three *cellae* in this narrow street. Therefore, although prostitution was in very close proximity to the elite household, that household was structured to disassociate itself from the sites of prostitution. The physical distance between the elite and the *infames* in Pompeii was not great, but the elite distanced themselves from the *infames* through their control over urban space. In other words, the elite structured their environment to distance themselves from those associated with *infamia* without creating zones, which created a physical distance between themselves and the rest of the population of the city. Instead, brothels in the city were situated in the narrower streets, in which there were few main entrances into *atrium* houses. This placed the prostitute out of sight of those arriving to dine with other morally respectable people, in particular wives and unmarried daughters, at the main entrance to houses. For visitors to arrive at the households of other members of the elite and to be confronted by the visibly deviant behaviour of the prostitute would have compromised the moral values of both the occupant of the house and the visitors. Therefore, brothels were situated in narrow streets, away from the gaze of the elite, in areas of the city that tolerated prostitution. These areas were, in most cases, the narrow streets of the central area to the east of the forum.

It was not only the brothels that had to be hidden from the view of

Plate 5.2 A *cella* at 7.13.19

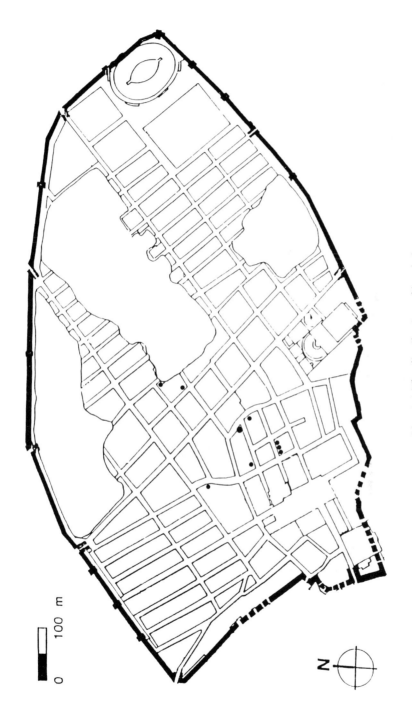

Map 5.1 The distribution of brothels

0 100 m

women and children secluded from the realities of city life. The prostitute was a regular feature of the bars and inns of the city. The legal definition of a prostitute given by Ulpian reveals the male attitude to women working in inns and bars: 'we would say that a woman openly practises prostitution not just where she does so in brothels but also where she is used to showing she has no shame in *cauponae* and other places' (Dig. 43, *praef.*). This statement establishes a connection between the *caupona* (inn) and the brothel, which can be in close proximity at Pompeii. For example, a bill for a man bringing produce to market shows that he was charged at an inn for wine, bread, gruel, a girl, and fodder for a mule (*CIL* 9.2689; MacMullen 1970; Frayn 1993). The connection between women who served at *cauponae* (inns) or *popinae* (bars) and prostitution was strongly expressed.

The cultural context expressed in literature does not suggest that there was a strong differentiation of places that served drink. The *popinae* were also associated with the sale of hot food, but the sources do not state that other places such as the *cauponae* did not serve hot food. The *cauponae* also provided accommodation, but it is possible that for the inhabitants of the city there may not have been a clear distinction between a *caupona* and a *popina*.

In the literary sources, there is a sharp contrast between the *popinae* and *cauponae* of the city and inns in the countryside. The country inns were respectable places where travellers stayed (Hor., *Sat.* 1.5). However, the city tavern, and particularly the *popina*, was attacked in literature as a place associated with drunkenness, singing, fighting and odious smells from the cooking of food to enable the drunk to drink more (Petr., *Sat.* 95; Hor., *Sat.* 2.4.62, *Epist.* 1.17; Propert. 8.19; Aus., *Mos.* 1.24; Sid.Apoll. 8.11.3.42). In reality, the *popinae* offered the facilities that aided sociability and conviviality. These features can be found in the archaeological evidence from Pompeii. The *popinae* at Pompeii were relatively small structures set up for the sale of food and drink. The *popina* at 9.11.2 highlights these features: at the front, there is a bar, in which are set *dolia* from which wine was drawn (*NS* 1912: 112–20). At the end of the bar counter there is a small stove. In the oven a small pastry dish was found, implying that snacks were served. A number of vessels were found on the counter, which probably contained food; the walls were decorated simply with whitewash, and behind the bar a number of *amphorae* were found. The *popina* would have been lit by a hanging lamp to allow it to open in the evening so that the customer could drink through the night because the *popina* did not close (Amm.Marc. 14.6.25; Propert. 4.8.2; Petr., *Sat.* 92; Juv. 8.158). Fifty-seven bronze coins and five silver coins were found in the *popina* at 9.11.2. A dice box was found on the upper floor, which demonstrates the connection between this *popina* and gambling. In literature, the customer was made to fit the moral environment of the *popinae* and was assumed to have been the thief, the gambler, the hangman, the coffin maker, the *gallus* or the bargeman (Plaut.,

Plate 5.3 A bar counter

Trin. 1021; Juv. 8.171; Amm.Marc. 14.6.25: on this passage see Matthews 1989: 414–16). Some of these types appear upon the walls of *popinae* and *cauponae* at Pompeii (Todd 1939). Similarly, the proprietor's morality matched their environment and their customers' morals; often they sell diluted wine as undiluted, and the owner of a *caupona* often appears in dreams murdering the customers (Cic., *Divin.* 1.57; Petr. 95.8; Mart. *Ep.*1.5.4, 1.56, 3.57). Thus, these drinking establishments were not places for respectable people even to set foot in (Hermansen 1981: 196; cf. Victorian England, Walvin 1978: 35–40).

In contrast, in the *Copa*, Surisca, a female server at a *caupona*, describes the facilities available inside to potential customers. To emphasise her points she girates to the noise of her castanets. Inside the *caupona* were the attractions of gardens, music, wine, garlanded rooms, a wide variety of food, and not least, girls (Pseud.Ver., *Copa*). Jashemski (1964) has highlighted how this image in the *Copa* mirrors the material evidence from Pompeii. For example, the largest *caupona*, at 7.11.11/14, displays many of these characteristics. There was accommodation for fifty guests; there was a small garden for the relaxation of guests, and to the rear a larger garden laid out for producing food for the *caupona*. A *triclinium* had been set up in what had once been the *atrium* of the house. On the ground floor and the upper floor were rooms for guests (Ruddell 1964: 105–6; Jashemski 1964: 344–6). However, the writer of the *Copa* still describes such a *caupona* as smoky. The large *caupona* at Pompeii was not located in the most morally correct part of town: its main entrance was opposite the city's largest brothel. However, it was located in close proximity to the *macellum* and forum, which would have been of considerable convenience for traders arriving for the weekly market in the city (Frayn 1993: 38–42). Therefore, if we penetrate the moral assumptions of the literary sources, it is possible to see in the *cauponae* many elements of popular entertainment available for the traveller: the provision of food and drink, singing, gambling, and a furnished place for social activity. That such places were centres for social activity is shown by Juvenal's comment that the *caupona* and *compitum* were both associated with gossip (Juv. 9.102; Hermansen 1981 notes that 20 per cent of identified taverns in Ostia were located on street corners). A further attribute of, certainly, the *cauponae*, but also of the *popinae*, was prostitution. The Digest suggests that any woman working in or even entering a *caupona* was potentially a prostitute and that the laws against rape and adultery could not be implemented (Dig. 23.2.43, *praef.*, 23.2.9, 3.2.4.2). This suggests that the *popinae* were centres for male rather than female entertainment. Also, if a person was summoned to appear at a *popina* or a brothel, they could state that these places were unsuitable and refuse to appear (Dig. 4.8.21.11). This link between the culture of the *popina* and the brothel in Roman law should not be seen as accidental. There was a distinction between the morally good elite and the rest of the population. This is important, because the elite controlled, managed and enforced the law and imposed their will upon the population of the city.

The attitude of the elite to the parts of the city associated with the *popina* and the brothel is summed up in the way they attack their opponents. These people were characterised as deviant by the author, who was, of course, morally correct. These attitudes appear in rhetoric: for example Cicero attacks Antony, in the *Philippics*, for wasting his life in brothels and *popinae*, in gambling and drinking. Aulus Gellius tells us that Cicero used such devices to indicate the sordidness of Antony's lifestyle (Gell. 6.4; Cic., *Phil.* 13.24; cf. Cic., *Pis.* 13 for an attack upon Piso emerging from a *popina* at the fifth hour; see also Suet., *Gramm.* 15). Again the connection between the *popinae* and the brothel is made. In the imperial period Nero and Vitellius were attacked by the historians for entering *popinae*. A general and a consul were also attacked by Juvenal for being resident in a *caupona* and a *popina* (for Nero see Suet., *Nero* 26; Tac., *Ann.* 13.25, 14.15; Dio 61.8. For Vitellius see Suet., *Vit.* 13; Juv. 8.146–63,171).

In the imperial period there was a concerted effort to control the form and nature of the *popinae* at Rome. The sources report an attack upon the *popinae*; however, the details are limited and only refer to the enforcement of restrictions on popular culture in the city of Rome. There is no record of a direct attack on the culture of the *popina* under Augustus, but Quintilian notes that when Augustus saw an *eques* eating at the games, he sent him a note saying 'If I want to dine, I go home' (Quint. 6.3.63). To eat in public was morally reprehensible. The first known restriction upon popular culture at Rome appeared under Tiberius, when in the context of other sumptuary measures, instructions were given to the aediles in Rome to forbid the sale of all food including pastries from the *popinae* and *ganeae* (Suet., *Tib*. 34). These measures do not seem to have lasted, and under Claudius a series of measures were introduced: the *collegia* set up by Gaius were to be disbanded, some taverns were closed, and the sale of meat and hot water was prohibited (Dio 60.6.7; Philo, *Leg*. 311–12). Further, the butchers and *vinarii* were not allowed to sell cooked meat as they used to (Suet., *Claud*. 38–40). Nero extended these restrictions to include the sale of all food with the exception of vegetables and pulses (Suet., *Nero* 16.2; Dio 62.14.2). These restrictions on meat consumption appear to be part of sumptuary laws. Vespasian further restricted the food available to pulses only (Dio 65.10.3). Such regulations were probably never enforced in Pompeii. However, they do reveal the cultural values of the capital, which may have made an impression on the aediles of Pompeii.

The total distribution of *cauponae* and *popinae* at Pompeii provides a further indication of those areas that formed deviant street networks (for *cauponae* and *popinae* see Ruddell 1964; Kleberg 1957; Jashemski 1979; Packer 1978). The *cauponae* tended to be situated near the gates of the city, in particular Porta di Stabia and Porta di Ercolano. Other gates are not surrounded by such a concentration of places for the visitor to spend the night, which might suggest that communications through the city were predominantly by these two gates. The other major concentration of *cauponae* where visitors could spend the night was located in *Regio 7* to the east of the forum. At the centre of this group of *cauponae* was the large brothel at 7.12.18/19. However, it would have been likely that the other *cauponae* were in close proximity to prostitution. The *cauponae* close to the gates of the city were not far from the tombs outside, a place of the prostitute in the literary sources, as we saw earlier. Other *cauponae* were close to the city walls, another place associated with the prostitute. Those *cauponae* located near the amphitheatre were near an ideal spot for the prostitute whilst the public building was not in use. In fact, the *cauponae* of the city seem to have been located away from those areas that were predominantly residential. This would seem to place the visitors to the city at the margins, unless they were staying at the *cauponae* close to the city's main brothel.

The *popinae* appear to have been fairly evenly spread throughout the city. There appears to have been a strong preference for a location upon the

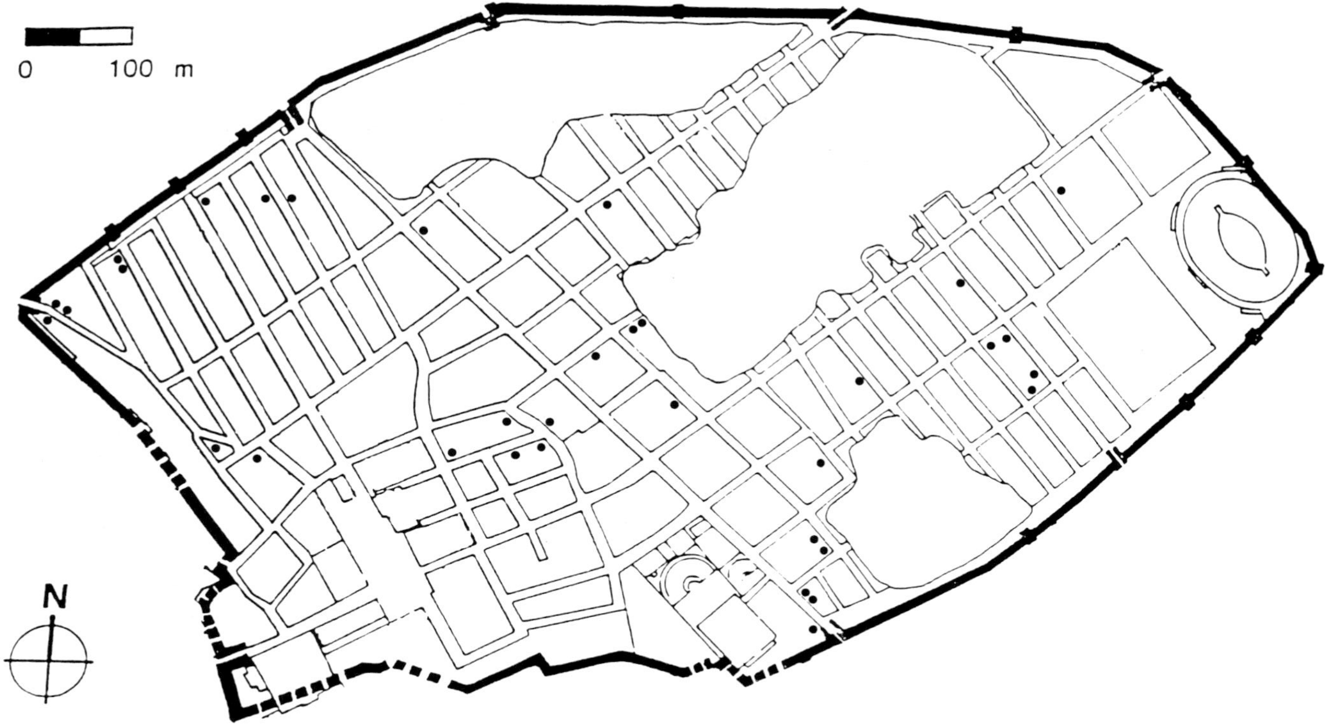

Map 5.2 The distribution of *cauponae*

100 m

0

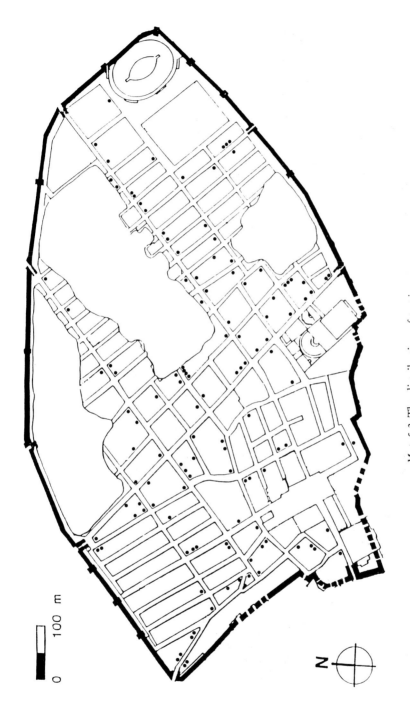

Map 5.3 The distribution of *popinae*

through-routes leading from the gates of the city. There were some areas in which there were relatively few *popinae* (Wallace-Hadrill 1994), including the forum, most of *Regio* 8, the section of Via dell'Abbondanza from the forum to its junction with Via di Stabia, those parts of *Regio* 6 that did not form a through-route, a section of Via della Fortuna from the temple of *Fortunae Augustae* to the junction with Vicolo di Storto, and parts of *Regio* 1. The common factor linking these places is that they are locations of the larger houses in the city, many of which were isolated from the *popinae*. This becomes relevant in the evening. At the ninth hour of daylight, the elite would have dined with their guests. After dinner, there may have been some form of entertainment (Mart. 4.8). This could well delay the guests until it was getting dark, when they would have departed into the street and been carried home in a litter with an escort (Juv. 3.280–8). If this street had been associated with *popinae*, the guests would have come into very close contact with this morally unacceptable *clientele*. For the elite, a home located away from moral corruption was an advantage. Also in the evening, as it was getting dark, the proprietors of the *popinae* would have lit lamps, which would penetrate the gloom of the streets. Streets without *popinae* in them would have been dark and quiet at night, whereas those associated with the *popinae* would have been distinguished by activity. On Map 5.4, the streets with *popinae* and *cauponae* in them have been shaded to illustrate this difference, the shaded areas representing those parts of the city in which social activity occurred in the late evening. The areas outside of this orbit of activity would have been dark and potentially perilous to walk through without an escort (Juv. 3.268–301; Apul., *Met.* 2.32; Petr. 79). However, these were also the areas in which members of the elite entertained or visited in the privacy of the home. This marks a major difference in the lives of the elite: their eating and drinking took place in private with a few selected persons, whereas for others drinking and eating occurred in public at the *cauponae* or the *popinae*.

Gambling was a feature of the *popinae*, and was an activity in which both the urban elite and others participated. Gambling was consistently attacked by members of the urban elite. This attack appears in rhetoric, as a means to discredit an opponent or their supporters. Typically, such an attack would link gambling with drinking and passing time in *popinae* and brothels (Macr., Sat. 3.16.14; Cic., *Phil.* 2.56, 2.67, 13.24, *Cat.* 2.10, 2.23).[2] Juvenal (11.176, 14.4) contrasts the different attitudes to the gambler and states that if a man was a member of the elite his gambling was regarded as an attribute, whereas if he was poor and gambled it was regarded as shameful and deviant. The type of gambling is not explicit. If it was at dice or knucklebones the activity would be illegal except at the *Saturnalia* (Mart., *Ep.* 4.14, 5.84, 14.13; Plaut., *Mil.* 164), but betting on horses and chariots was legal throughout the year (see Balsdon 1969: 151–9). This law appears to have been disregarded. Betting on dice was particularly associated with the

Map 5.4 Deviant streets

popinae. It was an activity that was regarded as a defect in a slave. The association of betting with drinking was common (Colum. 1.8.1–2; Dig. 21.19.1, 21.25.6; Tac., *Germ.* 24; Plaut., *Curc.* 355). In law, persons excluded from redress in the law of sale were gamblers, wine gluttons, impostors, liars and the quarrelsome (Dig. 21.1.4.2). Also, a person would have regarded himself as insulted if someone had taken his slave or his son into a *popina* or had played dice with him (Dig. 47.10.26). The gambler in comedy was associated with the criminal, and Plautus gives a fictional account of dice being played after a meal in a *popina*. The stakes were a cloak and a mantle; however, before the conclusion of the game one of the players passed out and was robbed by his opponent of his ring (Plaut., *Curc.* 355). A similar scene of dice playing appears on a wall painting in a *caupona* at Pompeii (*CIL* 4.3494; Todd 1939). An argument erupts over a dice throw, insults are exchanged, and the pair come to blows. The innkeeper removes the conflict to the pavement outside. Obviously, gambling often resulted in disputes of a violent nature. Roman law reflected this situation: a series of laws ceased to apply if gambling took place on the premises, and the owner or manager could not bring a charge of theft or assault if gambling took place. However, the gamblers themselves could bring actions for assault or theft, and thus gain redress in law (Dig. 11.5.1). More than anything, this seems to have been aimed at encouraging proprietors of *popinae* not to permit gambling on their premises.

Therefore, a number of laws ceased to apply in the *popinae* or *cauponae*. These included the laws against rape and adultery and, also, assault and theft if gambling was allowed to take place. All these restrictions on the application of the law seem to have been part of an attack on the culture of the *popinae*, with the hope that women would not work in them and that gambling would be discouraged. In spite of these measures it seems that gambling continued as a feature of the *popinae*, and it was recognised that gambling was the activity in which some of the firmest friendships were made (Amm.Marc. 28.4.21). Given the restrictions in the application of the law, in the context of the *popinae* and *cauponae*, the distribution of *popinae* and *cauponae* reflects a male rather than a female pattern of leisure. Thus, the *popinae* and *cauponae* provided a social context for public interaction, entertainment, and pleasure for men, with their emphasis upon drink, food, sex and gambling, as well as being a place to entertain friends. This public social interaction was frowned upon by the elite, with their emphasis upon entertainment at home or at a friend's house in private. Therefore, the elite labelled the *popinae* and *cauponae* as deviant. However, in reality, social interaction at the *popinae* or *cauponae* would have been a normal experience in city life and a key characteristic of the city.

In Pompeii, there were a number of areas that had a strong association with deviance. In the case of prostitution, this was concentrated in the deviant street network to the east of the forum in *Regio 7* and in those areas in close proximity to the gates of the city and public buildings. In contrast, the *popinae* were spread throughout the city, but were normally located away from the larger houses of the elite. This highlights the need of the elite to shelter their wives and children from contact with deviants. Women and children were zoned into domesticity in Pompeii (cf. Wilson 1991). To be morally correct the elite isolated themselves from the rest of the population of the city, whilst still being in close proximity to it. This was the elite's response to deviant behaviour, which ordered the potentially chaotic urban environment and perpetuated the image of the city as a place in which chaos was held at bay (Cohen 1985: 206–7).

6

STREET ACTIVITY AND
PUBLIC INTERACTION

The doorway of a house had an important role in describing the resident's status and what was inside the house. This role was enshrined around the god Janus, associated with the beginning of events (Ovid, *Fasti* 2.51; Cic., *Nat. Deor.* 2.67). The doorway was thought to mark the division between two types of air, one inside the house and the other outside in the street (Lucr. 4.29). Also the door marked the division between private and public space, and could be guarded by a porter (Ovid, *Fasti* 1.135; see Wallace-Hadrill 1988 on the levels of privacy in the Roman house). The doorway was the entrance into the house not only for people, but also for curses and diseases (Plin., *N.H.* 32.44; 28.86). A door could also shut in rumour (Catull. 67) and was seen to protect the virtue of women from strangers' attention (Apul., *Met.* 9.5; Hor., *Carm.* 1.25). The doorways of the famous could reflect their glory. These doorways would have been decorated to emphasise a person's achievements. For example, Augustus' door posts were wreathed with bay leaves (*R.G.* 34; Juv. 12.80–102; Petron. 28–9), and the consuls of 509 BC were permitted to have their doors opening into the street (Plin., *N.H.* 36.112). It would appear that in Rome it was normal to keep the main doors of houses open during the day, with a porter to control access to the house (Liv. 5.13.6–7; 6.25.9; Plaut., *Asin.* 273; Wallace-Hadrill 1988: 46). However, it is uncertain whether this was universal. It seems more likely that only the wealthy could afford the luxury of leaving their doors open. For others the door provided protection against burglars (Apul., *Met.* 1.11; 3.5). The ability to leave the door open allowed for the display of the status of the occupier. The onlooker in the street would have been presented with a visual narrative through the house, which would have provided information about the occupier's status (Watts 1987: 187). However, in times of crisis, even the most wealthy had to bolt their doors against attack (Cic., *Vat.* 22, Bibulus was driven from public spaces into the privacy of his house; cf. Cic., *Mil.* 18 for Pompey, or Cic., *Verr.* 2.69: Verres when governor in Sicily was besieged in a house; see Cic., *Cat.* 28 for Cicero; see also Tac., *Hist.* 1.33). The houses of the elite also had a side door that was not so strongly defended. During the looting of Cremona in AD 69, the Vitellian soldiers were particularly successful, because they knew where the side doors of the houses of the elite were (Dio 64.15). This suggests that the side entrances to houses were not easily identified. Equally, those doorways associated with shops or other retail outlets would have punctuated a person's journey through a street. Thus, the doorway was a noticeable feature of the Roman street. Also, the doorway marks the meeting point of space and the built environment, and the interface between public and private.

The placement of doorways and the use of street frontages would seem to reflect how the urban environment was used. For example, in a main street, there would have been a tendency for the maximisation of street frontages. In contrast, in a side street, the use of the street frontage would have reflected the lower incidence of activity. Therefore, the number of doorways opening into a street directly reflects the level of social activity and interaction that occurred in the street.

To analyse this phenomenon in Pompeii, a simple method was devised to measure the occurrence of doorways in a street. The number of doorways was counted in all streets. To allow for comparison between streets the figures for the number of doorways in streets had to be calibrated. This was simply done to reflect the occurrence of doorways in metres. The length of the streets was measured and the following simple formula was used:

$$\text{Occurrence of doorways} = \frac{\text{length of street in metres}}{\text{number of doorways}}$$

Some of the longer streets were divided into sections to gain a more representative sample that was of a similar size to the rest of the streets. For example, Via dell'Abbondanza was divided into four similar sample lengths: the first from the forum to the junction with Via di Stabia, the second from the junction to *Insula* 3.1, the third from *Insula* 3.1 to *Insula* 3.6 and the fourth from *Insula* 3.6 to Porta di Sarno. Via di Nola was also split in this case into two sections: the first from Via di Stabia to *Insula* 5.4 and the second from *Insula* 5.4 to Porta di Nola. Similarly, Via di Stabia was divided into two sections: one from Porta di Stabia to the junction with Via dell'Abbondanza, and the second from this junction to the intersection with Via di Nola.

This methodology resulted in a measurement of doorway occurrence in all of the excavated streets from Pompeii. The range of values for the occurrence of doorways was between every 2.1m and 127.0m. The median occurrence of doorways was every 7.3m. For the purposes of data presentation, these data are divided into four groups. The first includes streets with doorways occurring between every 0 and 5 metres, the second with doorways occurring between every 6 and 10 metres, the third with doorways occurring every 11–15 metres and the fourth with doorways occurring less often than every 15 metres. This data set is plotted as Maps 6.1–6.4. If we

Plate 6.1 Via di Nola: high occurrence of doorways

Plate 6.2 Vicolo degli Scheletri: low occurrence of doorways

examine the spatial distribution of streets with different incidences of door-ways, we find a pattern emerging.

To deal with the first group of streets, with doorways occurring more frequently than every 6 metres (Map 6.1), this group can be divided into two sets. The first has doorways occurring more frequently than every 3.0 metres, and the second has doorways occurring every 3.1–6.0 metres. To deal with the first set of streets, those in which doorways occur between every 2.1 and 3.0m: these streets were found to be routes directly connected to the forum or major through-routes, or a combination of the two. Streets exclusively connected to the forum included Via del Foro, Via delle Scuole and Via degli Augustali with an extension to include the street between *Insulae* 9.3 and 9.2. Also, within this group were the through-routes leading from the following gates: Stabia, Ercolano and Nola. Although its value is lower, we should also include Via Marina in this group. This is caused by its proximity to the basilica and the temple of Venus, which are public buildings and do not have doorways at the usual frequency. It is of particular note that the values in this group on through-routes tail off to the east, for instance along Via dell'Abbondanza, but not on Via di Nola. This group defines the major through-routes. Via di Vesuvio should also be included in this group, although it falls just outside our artificial division into categories, and the higher value may be due to the fact that two streets lead to the Porta Vesuvio, reducing the concentration of traffic on both those routes by 50 per cent.

If we now examine the group of streets with doorways occurring between 3.1m and 6.0m we find that these are located predominantly to the east of the forum and to the west of Via di Stabia. An exception is Vicolo degli Scheletri, which has a much lower occurrence of doorways. Its value is created by the fact that there was very high activity occurring in the streets on the other side of the *insula* blocks backing on to it. In other words, it is in Vicolo degli Scheletri that there were few entrances, because houses in these *insulae* were entered from other streets. This also made Vicolo degli Scheletri an ideal street for the location of prostitution, as we saw in Chapter 5. However, the rest of this area forms a zone of high activity, and should be associated with the central core of the city. This zone should be seen as an area that adjoins the forum, and therefore as a transition zone between the forum (*CBD*) and the rest of the city. After all, it is in this area that there was a strong concentration of inns, bakeries, workshops and brothels as com-pared with other areas of the city. Other streets with doorways occurring between every 3.1 and 6.0m include Via di Mercurio, which can be seen to be a northward extension from the forum, and is a wider street than those found elsewhere in *Regio* 6 with a north–south orientation. There is another group of streets around the area of the theatre complex that has values in the 3.1–6.0m range, two of which form a route from Via dell'Abbondanza to a point on Via di Stabia near the theatres. It should be noted that higher levels

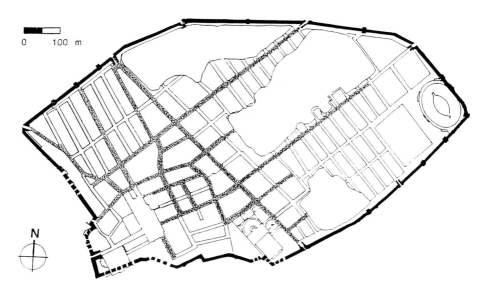

Map 6.1 Occurrence of doorways every 0–5 metres

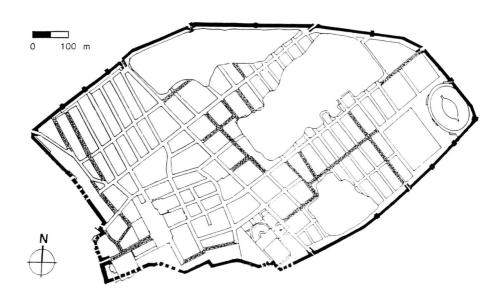

Map 6.2 Occurrence of doorways every 6–10 metres

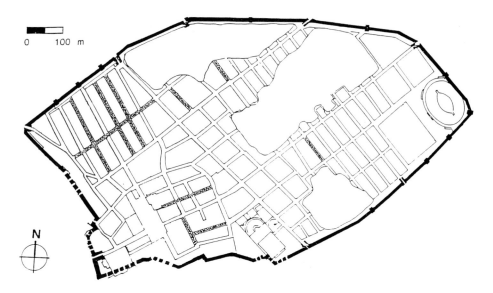

Map 6.3 Occurrence of doorways every 11–15 metres

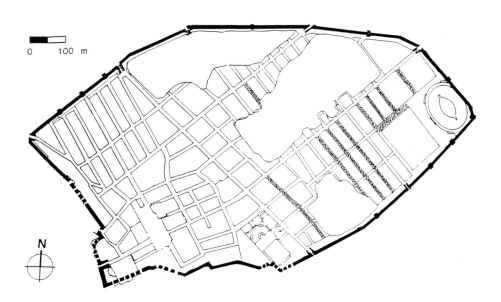

Map 6.4 Occurrence of doorways less than every 15 metres

of activity would have been expected here, because Via dei Teatri leads from Via dell'Abbondanza to the triangular forum, the republican bath complex, the temple of Isis and the theatres. The other two streets in this group are found adjoining Via di Stabia. These include Via del Menandro, which was associated with a number of craft workshops, and Vicolo del Conciapelle, which was in close vicinity to some of the city's inns. Thus, the streets with an occurrence of doorways more frequent than one every 6.0 metres are in the following areas: to the east of the forum, Via di Mercurio to the north of the forum, Via delle Scuole to the south of the forum, the through-routes of the city leading to gates, and the areas off Via di Stabia.

The next category of analysis consists of those streets with doorways occurring less often than every 6.0 metres, but more often than every 11.0 metres (see Map 6.2). This group includes the street leading from Porta di Nocera and the streets that form a direct route from the amphitheatre to Via di Stabia. The level of activity in these streets may have a direct relationship to the influence of the amphitheatre on the rest of the urban structure. The nature of activity in the amphitheatre was sporadic, with a high density of interaction occurring when it was functioning, and a low level of activity when it was not. Thus, the direct routes to the amphitheatre experienced similar fluctuations in activity and, as a result, do not have the higher incidences of doorways found on the through-routes, in Via dell'Abbondanza, for example. Also in this category are those streets to the west of the forum and those streets not on through-routes to the east of Via di Stabia. It should be noted that the occurrence of doorways declines the further to the east the street is. A similar pattern occurs in the regions to the north and south of the central area. Thus, this group includes all of those streets that did not form through-routes, but were in close proximity to the through-routes or close to areas that were associated with high levels of activity.

The third category comprises those streets that have a doorway occurring less often than every 11 metres but more often than every 15 metres (see Map 6.3). These streets tend to be associated with areas in the west of the city with reasonably high levels of activity. However, because there was a preference for entering *insulae* from other streets, such as Via di Mercurio, the streets in this third category, for example Vicolo della Fullonica, did not have high occurrences of doorways. Equally, the level of social interaction in these streets was also much lower. It should be noted that one narrow street in this group, Vicolo di Tesmo, does form a route that joins Via delle Consolare with Via di Vesuvio and Vicolo dei Vettii. However, it did not develop as a route associated with high levels of activity, because it was isolated from the major areas of activity in the city.

The fourth category includes all those streets with doorway occurrences that are less frequent than every 15 metres (see Map 6.4). These streets are exclusively in the south-eastern part of the city, which was associated with a

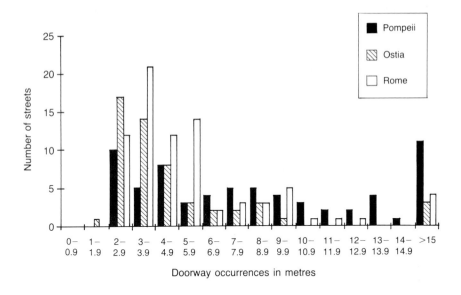

Figure 6.1 Streets in Pompeii, Ostia and Rome

lower density of land use, which included agricultural plots, as we saw in Chapter 4. These streets were isolated from the social interaction associated with the rest of the city.

To allow for comparison of the pattern of social interaction in streets, as defined by the occurrence of doorways, similar analysis was conducted upon excavated streets from Ostia and streets on the *Forma Urbis Marmorea* from Rome (Rodriguez-Almeida 1980). The data from Ostia revealed a much higher occurrence of doorways in most streets, with a median occurrence of doorways at every 3.2m, whereas Pompeii's median occurrence of doorways was every 7.3m. The data from the *Forma Urbis Marmorea* provide further data for comparison with Pompeii. The three data sets include a similar number of streets. The number of streets within 1.0 metre categories of doorway occurrence is plotted for the three cites, as Figure 6.1, and this shows the extent of variation in the amount of interaction in the streets. The data from Pompeii display the widest degree of variation, which would suggest that the infrastructure allowed a degree of freedom in the types of human behaviour that could be achieved in the urban environment of Pompeii. In other words, there were streets with intense social interaction and other streets with a less pronounced frequency of activity. In contrast, the data set from Ostia pointed to very intense levels of social activity throughout the city. This is partially caused by the nature of excavated streets at Ostia. They are for the most part through-routes, which might suggest that activity would have been concentrated upon them. The data from Rome, not surprisingly, pointed to a more intense level of social activity in most of the streets. The lower intensity of activity in some of the streets in Pompeii can be accounted for with reference to the density of settlement in the city. Ostia, unlike Pompeii, was a city of apartment blocks, which were designed to utilise space to the maximum. In contrast, the urban fabric of Pompeii consisted of a form of low-rise housing that had been developed by the owners with little reference to the ideals of design so apparent in Ostia (for Ostia see Meiggs 1973; Hermansen 1978; 1981; Packer 1971).

A second method of analysis was designed as a check on the assumption underlying the analysis of the occurrence of doorways, namely that the number of doorways reflected the relevant levels of activity in a street. The methodology is very similar to that for the measurement of doorway occurrences. The graffiti were counted and the length of the streets was used to calculate the occurrence of graffiti in a street. The following equation was used to do this:

$$\text{Occurrence of messages} = \frac{\text{the length of the street}}{\text{number of messages}}$$

The major problem with the second methodology is that it can only be used in the analysis of Pompeii, and can be seen entirely as a function of the unique data set available from Pompeii. However, even this data set is erratically recorded, and is dependent upon a variety of excavation and recording techniques (Mouritsen 1988: 47–52). For example, the excavations from the twentieth century pin-point the position of graffiti, but previous to this the graffiti were recorded erratically, with the result that the location of street messages in Via delle Consolare in many cases is unclear, even to the point where it is uncertain whether a graffito was written inside or outside of a building. Nevertheless, the variation of recorded occurrences of graffiti through the city does not appear to be that great. The data set has a range of graffiti occurring in streets from every 0.4m to every 258.0m. The pattern emulates the spatial distribution, which was established from the examination of the occurrence of doorways in streets.

However, there are a number of significant differences. These highlight the interaction of those travelling through the streets rather than localised patterns of social interaction within the street. Streets with graffiti occurring every 4.0m or less (Map 6.5) can be defined as the through-routes of the city, which corresponds to the transport network. We should exclude from this transport network the section of Via dell'Abbondanza from the forum to Via di Stabia, because it was blocked to wheeled traffic. The rest of this group represents all those streets that lead to a gate, including the street leading north between *Insulae* 5.3 and 5.4 to the Porta di Capua, and the streets leading to Porta Ercolano and Porta di Marina (here the values fall outside our category; but this is likely to be a direct result of inadequate recording in early excavations). Also in this category are those streets that join two major through-routes, for example Vicolo di Mercurio, which connects Via delle Consolare with Via di Vesuvio. In our examination of the occurrence of doorways, these streets do not appear to exhibit high levels of activity, because the occurrence of doorways was not frequent. However, this fact is most revealing. These streets have a higher occurrence of street messages for the simple reason that there are fewer doorways in the street, which leaves a greater wall area on which to place graffiti. The placement of graffiti upon the walls of streets with few doorways suggests that these streets would form part of a network of streets in which movement rather than social interaction was emphasised. Others include the streets connecting Via di Stabia directly to the amphitheatre, Vicolo di Tesmo, Vicolo di Paquio Proculo, Vicolo di Nozze D'Argento, Vicolo delle Lupanare, the street between *Insulae* 2.3 and 2.4, the street between *Insulae* 9.1 and 9.2, and Vicolo di Balbo. The only street that does not connect up with a major through-route as defined by the occurrence of doorways is Via di Mercurio, which illustrates its exceptional importance in the urban form. It would seem likely that Via di Mercurio had a unique level of activity generated by its position in relationship to the forum, and that the properties on the street were mostly entered via a *fauces*.

Streets with values over 4.1 metres and under 8.0 metres form in most cases the streets of lesser activity and interaction, and generally did not lead to a gate (see Map 6.6). However, many of these streets were primary transport routes. They include Via di Nocera, the north–south route through the central zone of the city to the east of the forum. The inclusion of Via delle Consolare, Via di Nola and Via delle Marina in this group can be accounted for because the graffiti in these streets were erratically recorded by the excavators.

The third category of streets, which has messages occurring every 8.1–12.0 metres, is particularly small (Map 6.7) and will be considered with the fourth category, composed of those streets with messages occurring less often than every 12 metres (see Map 6.8). A number of the streets in these two categories can be accounted for because they were poorly recorded by the excavators. However, those streets to the south-east of the city have been particularly well recorded, but do not display high incidences of street messages. These streets were isolated from the through-routes of the city. Significantly, on the through-routes in the south-eastern part of the city message occurrence was frequent. It would appear from Maps 6.7 and 6.8 that streets isolated from the main urban areas of activity were avoided by the painters of street messages. This, in itself, is for the simple reason that messages in these streets would not have been seen, because these streets did not experience high levels of social activity.

Therefore, from the above study of the occurrence of street messages it

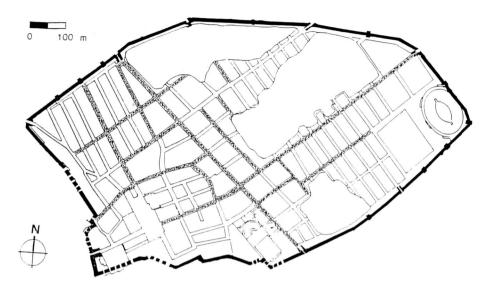

Map 6.5 Occurrence of messages every 0–4 metres

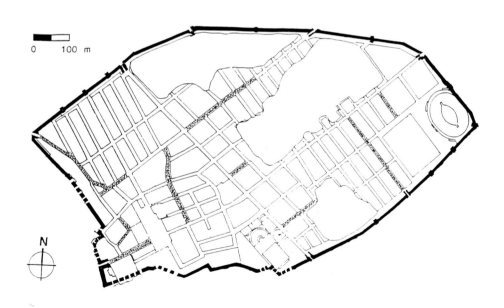

Map 6.6 Occurrence of messages every 4–8 metres

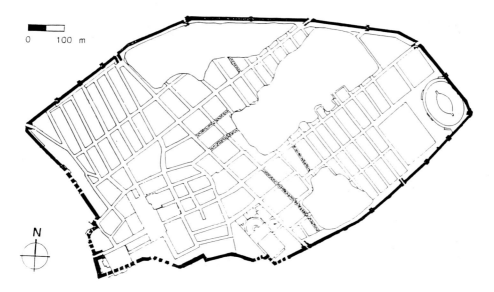

Map 6.7 Occurrence of messages every 8–12 metres

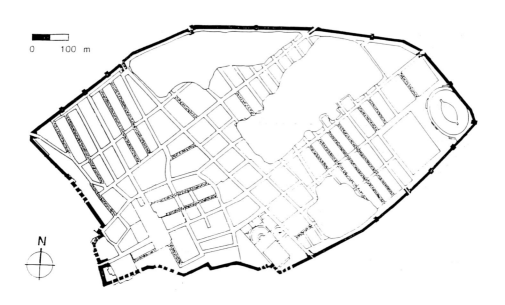

Map 6.8 Occurrence of messages less often than every 12 metres

may be concluded that the position and frequency of graffiti in streets reflects the higher levels of activity associated with those streets. Unlike the previous examination of doorway occurrences, this methodology highlights the activity of people who used a particular street, but who did not necessarily live in that street. Parts of the region to the east of the forum have a significantly lower incidence of message occurrence, because the streets have consistently high occurrences of doorways. Thus, there was often limited space for the display of graffiti. Also, some of these streets do not form major through-routes and, in consequence, may have been less attractive for the placement of street messages. In contrast, the areas that form through-routes tended to have a high frequency of messages occurring in them, as well as a high occurrence of doorways. It was primarily the streets that were transport routes through the city that were the most frequent locations for street-message placement. Such a pattern is also reflected in Mouritsen's distribution maps of the graffiti associated with individual candidates (Mouritsen 1988: 53–7). The graffiti were placed on walls without authorisation from the owner; therefore, their placement was at the discretion of their creator, and there is no conclusive evidence to associate the graffiti with the owners of property facing on to the various streets (Mouritsen 1988: 58–9). The fact that the graffiti tended to concentrate on the through-routes of the city suggests that these messages were intended to be read by people coming into the city, from the countryside, as well as people resident within the city walls. Thus, the distribution of graffiti reflects the incidence of inhabitants and strangers in the city of Pompeii.

To return to the study of doorways, we have already seen how some streets had higher occurrences of doorways in them. However, this methodology did not account for the variation of doorway types, or the variation in the use of street frontages. A doorway which was associated with a retail shop had a wide entrance looking on to the street. In contrast, the entrance to an *atrium* house was associated with a deep corridor, known as a *fauces*, that led into the house (see Plate 6.3). The *fauces* separated the *atrium* from the street, whereas the doorway associated with shops helped to integrate this part of the built environment with the street. Therefore, doorways can be categorised as either type 1, associated with the *fauces* of an *atrium* house, or type 2, associated with shops. To account for this variation in doorway type and use of street frontages, the two types of doorways are compared to ascertain whether some streets were dominated by shops or *atrium*-type houses. For the sake of comparison, this measurement is expressed as a ratio between type 1 and type 2 doorways. Because Pompeii was fundamentally a city of *atrium* houses, we might expect this factor to dominate the relationship between type 1 and type 2 doorways (Wallace-Hadrill 1990; Dwyer 1991). Ideally, this is characterised with a *fauces* flanked by two shops (see Plate 6.3). If this was the dominant pattern for the use of street frontages in Pompeii, we might expect a ratio of 1:2 (type 1: type 2). However, the ratios

Plate 6.3 Two different types of doorway: type 1 leading into the house and type 2 associated with the bar

ranged from 1:1 to 1:9 (Via dei Teatri, however, had no doorways of type 1). The mean was calculated at 1:3 and the median was 1:4, which should be taken as the normal experience in Pompeian streets. This would suggest that the ideal of a *fauces* flanked by two shops was not the dominant type in Pompeii. The data range from 1:1 to 1:9 is not as numerically wide as our previous two data sets. Therefore, when we make comparisons between streets, we do not need to divide the data into four sets. For the sake of presentation this data set is divided into two, one group of streets with a ratio higher than the median and another with a ratio less than the median (see Map 6.9). Some anomalies do arise in streets that have very few doorways and lower levels of activity, for example Vicolo della Fullonica. These anomalies are most common in *Regiones* 1 and 2. In the category of streets with a higher ratio than 1:4 were the streets that were defined by method 1 as the central area and the through-routes in the western part of the city. However, the through-routes in the eastern part of the city are only partially represented in this group. In Via dell'Abbondanza, to the east of Via di Stabia, the higher ratio only occurs near the Porta di Sarno. In the case

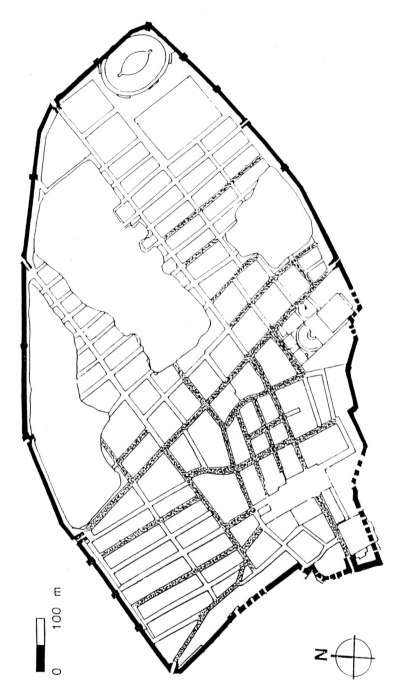

Map 6.9 Ratio of type 1:type 2 doorways (shading = a ratio of 1:4 to 1:9)

0   100   m

N

of the Via di Nola, a similar pattern is apparent. The lower ratios in the eastern part of the city would seem to reflect the dominance of the *atrium* house type in this area, with a *fauces* and flanked by two shops. These areas included *Regiones* 1, 2, 5, 6 and 9. We should also include the isolated parts of *Regiones* 7 and 8. It was in these areas that the *atrium* house was the more dominant housing type, whereas in the central area of the city and the through-routes in the western part of the city, other forms of urban fabric had a stronger presence. In this area, the retail shop took on a far more important role than in *Regiones* 1, 2, 5, 6 and 9. To see these areas, with their emphasis on the *atrium* house, as representative of all housing types in Pompeii is unrealistic (Wallace-Hadrill 1990 sees *Regiones* 1, 2 and 6 as a representative sample of the whole of Pompeii). There was a fundamental difference between the use of street frontages in these areas and the intensive use of street frontages in the central area of the city and through-routes of the western part of the city (this pattern is confirmed by a survey of wheel ruts undertaken by Tsujimura 1991).

To conclude this chapter, it would appear that the arrangement of streets in Pompeii had a certain logic which caused the variation in the number of doorways, message occurrence, and the ratio of type 1: type 2 doorways. Emphasis was laid upon the through-routes as the streets with the greatest competition for street frontage. This suggests that interaction occurred at a greater level in streets that were major routes in the transport network. The fact that these through-routes led from the city gates towards the centre of the city implies that the social relationship between inhabitant and stranger was stronger than that between inhabitant and inhabitant and that there was a high frequency of visitors to Pompeii. The through-routes with the highest incidence of usage were those that formed a north–south axis. This might suggest that Pompeii was placed on a north–south route for land transport, whereas the east–west route was dominated by water transport up the river Sarno. The major through-routes of the city were also marked by the shrines of the *Lares Compitales*, which defined the boundaries of the *vici*. It is notable that these through-routes were integrated at the core of the city in the area to the east of the forum in *Regio* 7. The separation of properties from the street was most pronounced in areas that were least integrated within the street network. These were also probably those areas in which the inhabitants had the greatest control over the internal space of their properties.

7

THE PRODUCTION OF SPACE

In Chapter 6 a pattern of street activity was established from a study of the use of the interface between the edges of the *insulae* and the street. To begin to account for this phenomenon it is necessary first to identify the spatial generators which produced the pattern of doorway occurrences in Pompeii. In effect, what are being analysed are those local factors which imposed controls upon what would otherwise be the random occurrence of doorways.

One of the controls upon randomness which has been observed to be present in many Roman cities was the grid plan. This factor has been observed by numerous scholars, but seldom analysed in spatial terms (see Haverfield 1913: 14; Ward-Perkins 1974: 33–6; Owens 1989: 14; contra Mumford 1961: 246; Rykwert 1976: 41–67 for an alternative). It has also been recognised that an *insula* block can only be divided in so many ways to produce *atrium*-type houses (Maiuri 1942). The approach adopted here is somewhat different. An *insula* block is normally a quadrilateral form that is defined by the street grid. In Pompeii, these *insulae* vary in shape from square through rectilinear to rhomboid. Ideally the positioning of doorways upon these blocks would either be random or form an even distribution, but any brief observation of the distribution of doorways upon an *insula* block will reveal that this distribution is anything but even or random. For example the *insula* block *Regio 7.14* has fourteen doorways on Via dell' Abbondanza, two doorways on Vicolo delle Lupanare, one on Vicolo degli Scheletri and three on Vicolo della Maschera. This would suggest that the dominant directional focus at a crude level was to the south on to Via dell'Abbondanza. However, in many cases such a procedure would not take into account the size of the street frontage. For example, some *insula* blocks have many doorways on their shortest side, but an equal number on their long side. Therefore, such a crude procedure of solely counting the doorways on each side of an *insula* block may not reveal the dominant direction in proportion to the amount of street frontage available. To avoid such distorted data the following method was adopted. Each *insula* block was measured, and the number of doorways was counted. Then this number of doorways was hypothetically distributed in an even pattern and the deviation of the real examples from this even distribution was measured. The exact controls which governed the siting and structure of Pompeian housing are far from self-evident: there would appear to be little overall planning of the forms of whole *insula* blocks, which might be attributed to the way in which these blocks have become subdivided over time.

However, there are two *insulae* which were planned as whole units, 7.5 and 9.4, which can be used as controls with which the other *insulae* can be compared. These two *insulae* contain respectively the forum baths and the central baths (Richardson 1988: 147–53, 286–9). By studying the layout of these two *insulae*, we see in their design a perception of use of the streets surrounding the *insulae*, and an appreciation by the designers of how these two *insulae* would be integrated into the extant street form.

The older of the two structures, 7.5, contains the forum baths. The faces of the *insula* are fairly evenly distributed round the circumference: 23 per cent face north, 18 per cent face south, 28 per cent face east and 30 per cent face west. If the building was designed to maximise use or to have an even pattern of use on all sides, these figures would be reflected in the proportions of doorways facing each direction. This is not the case: 28 per cent of the doorways face north, 14 per cent face south, 41 per cent face east and 17 per cent face west. The emphasis of the interface between the *insula* and its surrounding space is in an easterly direction, with another emphasis to the north. There would appear to be a designed directional pull away from the south and west. The main public entrances into the baths are also aligned on the north and east sides of the *insula*. Therefore, the person who designed the block was working within an already existing pattern of use of the areas around it, which emphasised the importance of Via delle Terme and Via del Foro. These are the major through-routes, whereas the other two streets performed a lesser role. It was these factors that were incorporated into the design of this *insula* block.

The *insula* containing the central baths, 9.4, has the following distribution of frontage around its circumference: 27 per cent face north, 23 per cent face east, 27 per cent face south and 23 per cent face west. The *insula* is approximately square, and if there was an even pattern of use, this would be reflected in an even distribution of doorways facing each direction. Again, this is not the case: 33 per cent of the doorways face north, 11 per cent face east, 6 per cent face south and 50 per cent face west. In this structure there was a strong directional pull away from the south and east to the west and the Via di Stabia, with only a minor positive deviation from the expected even pattern to the north. The building encroaches upon Vicolo di Tesmo on its east side and, as a result, this street is too narrow for wheeled traffic. This emphasises the lesser role played by this street in the structure of the building and the street pattern of Pompeii.

In these two examples, we see one of the fundamental structures of

Plate 7.1 Insula 9.4 from Via di Stabia

Plate 7.2 Insula 9.4 (right) from Vicolo di Tesmo

Roman urbanism being designed to utilise the space around it. This use of space is not a maximisation of the space available on all the frontages of the building, but only on those frontages through which people entered the structures. In both cases, these frontages coincide with the through-routes of the city, and the emphasis upon urban activity was towards the centre and the north of the city. The streets that were isolated by this emphasis of activity had a lesser role to play in the structure of the city; they were often narrower (compare Vicolo di Tesmo and Via di Nola), and were areas that would have been avoided by strangers, in favour of those streets that were wide and presented a vista into the distance. Thus the structure of even the most designed *insulae* took account of the extant patterns of street activity. These two examples of designed *insulae* set the context for the following analysis of the other *insula* blocks in Pompeii. All the *insulae* were examined to establish their directional focus, using the above methodology.

To unravel the considerable quantity of data, generated through the study of the façades of *insulae*, a series of maps is used to highlight the main features. First, the side of each *insula* block with the highest proportion of doorways is plotted (see Map 7.1). This map demonstrates that in most cases the directional focus is concentrated towards the through-routes. Interestingly, there is a marked difference of emphasis between *Regiones* 6 and 1. Although both contain *insulae* that are rectangular and of similar proportions, in all but one case in *Regio* 6 the highest proportion of doorways in an *insula* was on a longer side, while in *Regio* 1 the emphasis is on the shorter north side of the *insulae*. This is particularly marked when the *insulae* come into contact with Via dell'Abbondanza. In this *Regio* some blocks do have their strongest focus towards a longer side, but in all cases these were related to contact with Via di Nocera. *Regio* 1 illustrates the standard influence of the through-routes. In contrast, *Regio* 6 does not conform to this local constraint upon randomness. This can be accounted for with reference to Via di Mercurio, which, although it is not a through-route, displays all the attributes of a through-route in spatial terms: a high occurrence of doorways and a frequent occurrence of messages. Its uniqueness is also highlighted by the presence of an arch at its southern end. However, this cannot account fully for the pattern of the other streets in *Regio* 6. In other areas of the city there is no marked deviation from the expected pattern, in which the random or the even distribution of doorways is modified by a greater emphasis upon the through-routes.

This method of analysis, although crude, has revealed certain factors. To resolve some of the anomalies, and particularly those in *Regio* 6, the percentage of the total number of doorways on each side of the *insula* block was calculated. In many cases, the proportional differences between sides of *insulae* were not very great. This is particularly true of the area of *Regio* 7 to the east of the forum. There would appear to have been a strong directional pull away from Vicolo degli Scheletri. Two *insulae* (7.4 and 8.4) had a virtually

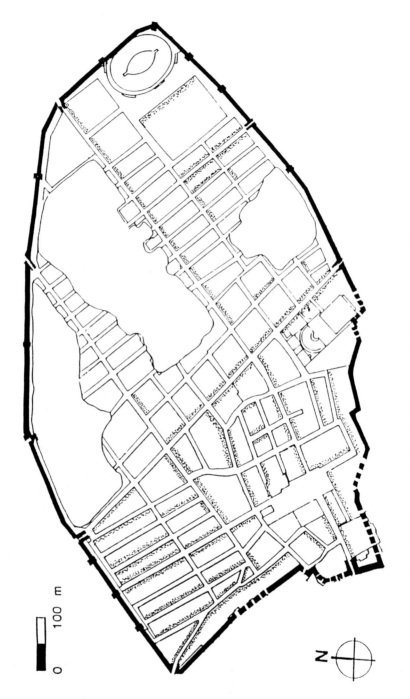

Map 7.1 Doorways in *insulae* (shading = the highest number of doorways)

even distribution of doorways around their circumferences, and it would seem that this can be explained with reference to their position. Both *insulae* were surrounded by through-routes and streets that connected through-routes. Thus, these two *insulae* were fully integrated into the street grid and maximised the use of their perimeter, whereas in all other *insulae*, certain sides had few doorways opening on them, and other sides were given a greater emphasis of use. Therefore, this method does not take us any further in attempting to understand the pattern of use of the façades of *insulae*. Instead, we have confirmed that the pattern of use was dominated by the relationship between the position of doorways on the sides of *insulae* and the location of the through-routes in the city.

To resolve this lack of definition, it was decided to plot positive deviation from an even pattern of doorway occurrence in *insulae*. This yielded some remarkable results (see Map 7.2). As expected, positive deviation from a random pattern was most marked when an *insula* came into contact with a through-route. This accounts for most of the positive deviation above 20 per cent. In *Regio* 6, *Insulae* 9, 11 and 14 approached an even pattern, for which it is hard to account. There was little positive deviation in *Regio* 7. However, the strongest positive deviation was shown in *Regio* 1. This seems to suggest that positive deviation from an even or random pattern occurs in areas in which the owners of property have the greatest control over how their property is entered from the street. In areas such as *Regiones* 6 and 7, where there is more pressure on space, the occurrence of doorways is less controlled by the owners of property. This would imply that there were a greater number of properties in *Regiones* 6 and 7 than in *Regiones* 1 and 2. This would appear to be one of the logical generators of the patterns of doorway occurrence identified in the previous chapter.

Therefore, the social relationship that would appear to cause the Pompeian spatial configuration was the relationship between inhabitants and strangers, or people from outside the city. This is demonstrated by the emphasis upon through-routes leading to the centre of the city. However, it would also appear that in some areas this relationship was suppressed, or masked by other relationships that were occurring. This is particularly true of the area of *Regio* 7 to the east of the forum and to a certain extent *Regio* 6.

The question why these areas mask the inhabitant–stranger relationship is not easily answered. Both areas are close to the forum. They have a significantly different arrangement of streets: *Regio* 6 has all the attributes of orthogonal planning, whereas *Regio* 7 is anything but regular in terms of street plan. Could the underlying logic of such a pattern be quite basic? Do regular and irregular street patterns in themselves produce very different spatial relationships?

We begin by examining the street plan (Map 7.3). Through-routes define the two areas of study. *Regio* 6 is defined by Via della Fortuna, Via delle Terme, Via di Stabia and Via delle Consolare. The second study area, the

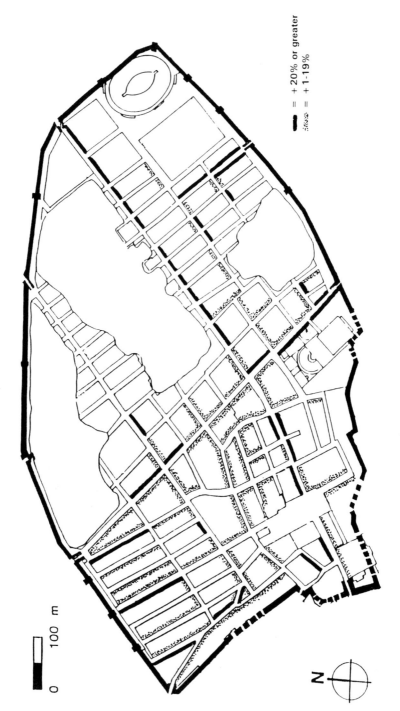

= + 20% or greater

= + 1-19%

Map 7.2 Deviation from expected pattern of doorway placement

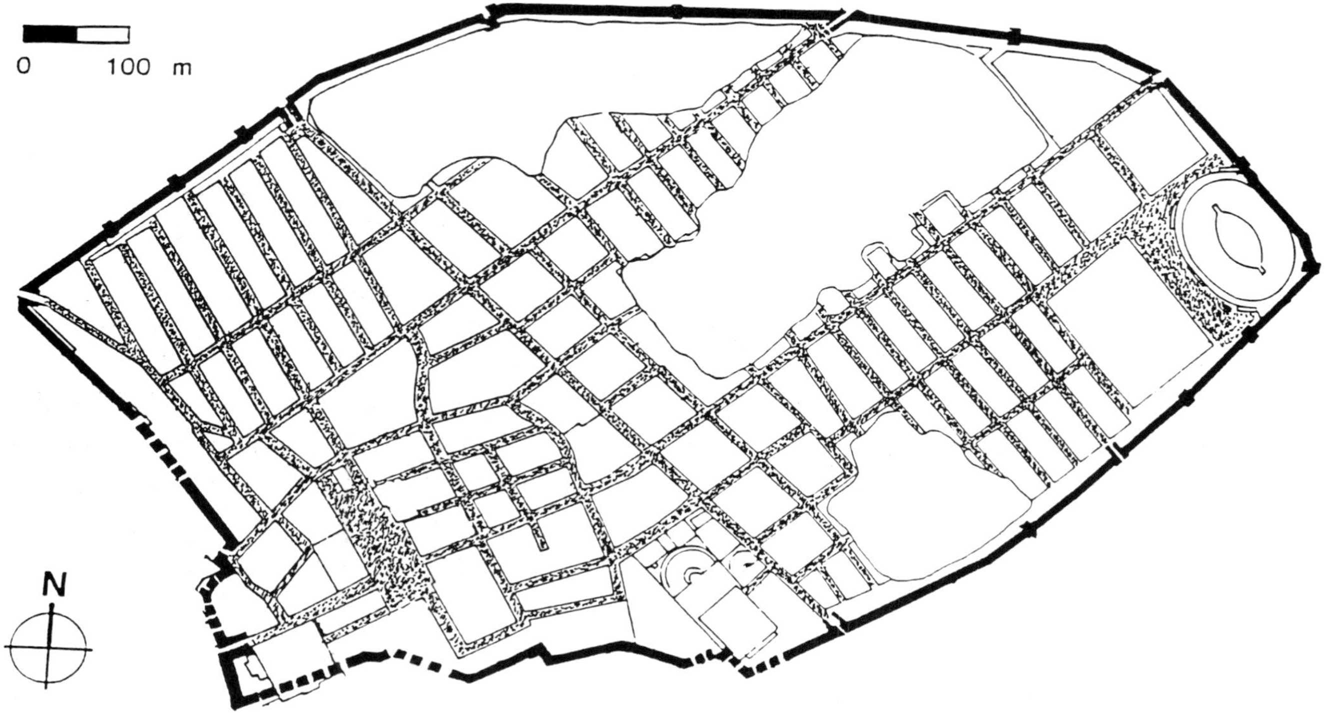

Map 7.3 The street network

100 m

0

part of *Regio* 7 to the east of the forum, is bounded by Via dell'Abbondanza, Via di Stabia, the forum and Via del Foro, and Via della Fortuna. Thus both areas would appear to be integrated into a network of through-routes.

However, *Regio* 6 would appear to have a very linear alignment. The streets appear to promote movement in a north–south direction, from and towards the through-route of Via della Fortuna/Via delle Terme. This would appear to be caused by the physical structure of the street, which would have drawn people to the vanishing point of the street, in those streets that lead from the south in a consistent northerly direction. The lateral street Vicolo di Mercurio would appear to play a lesser role, with a low occurrence of doorways upon it. However, its role as a communications channel is highlighted by the relatively high occurrence of messages in the street. The streets running north–south in this area are all dead ends beyond Vicolo di Mercurio. This factor in itself would isolate these areas from a stranger visiting the city. Few strangers utilise streets that do not connect with other streets unless there is a specific reason for them to visit that street, which is known in advance. This observation may be a key to comprehending the different spatial patterns displayed by *Regiones* 6 and 7. In many ways, *Regio* 6 is a non-distributive area, with the movement of people flowing around, rather than through, the area. This is illustrated further by the positioning of the arch at the southern end of Via di Mercurio. The arch would appear to be placed in such a manner as to form a boundary, but at the same time the arch draws a person's line of sight through it (MacDonald 1986: 75–87). The idea of a very permeable boundary is particularly significant, because there is a shrine of the *Lares* sited in Via di Mercurio (6.8.13). These shrines, as we have already seen, formed boundaries along the through-routes of Pompeii. Thus, *Regio* 6 would appear isolated from the inhabitant–stranger interface. Instead, the streets all lead into the central forum area, which suggests that an emphasis was placed upon the isolation of the area from strangers, and a greater emphasis upon the inhabitant–inhabitant interface.

Regio 7 is rather different. The streets and *insula* blocks are highly irregular in both size and shape. This would appear to reflect the antiquity of the area.[1] It would also seem to reflect organic rather than planned growth. An alternative explanation is that a grid had been set out, but had become totally deformed because of pressure to build structures that expanded beyond the confines of the *insula* block.[2] The form of *Regio* 7, upon destruction in AD 79, displays a mixture of orthogonal planning to the south with elements of informal growth to the north. For example, Vicolo di Storto and Vicolo delle Lupanare have pronounced curves. This mixture of informality and formality should not come as a surprise because, as Ward-Perkins (1974: 8–9) has pointed out, Roman cities usually display elements of formal and informal planning. As in the case of *Regio* 6 the through-routes tend to go around this area. However, as we saw in the previous chapter, there were high occurrences of doorways and street messages in this area. This suggests that the area was in some way integrated with the rest of the city. An explanation for this might be that this area formed a central area within the city, which integrated the through-routes with each other, whilst maintaining a strong relationship with the forum. Via degli Augustali forms a link between the forum and Via di Stabia, with a side branch, Vicolo delle Lupanare, to Via dell'Abbondanza. Vicolo di Eumachia and Vicolo di Storto establish a link between Via dell'Abbondanza and Via della Fortuna. Therefore, the central position of this area promotes movement through a series of rather complicated short cuts. For the total stranger such routes would remain undiscovered, but for the inhabitant or frequent visitor these routes provided rapid movement that avoided the circuitous through-routes. It is not so much the different street pattern of *Regio 7* that marks it out as different from *Regio 6*, but rather its position within the city.

These observations in many ways return us to the question of zoning in the Roman city. Although, in Chapter 1, the concept of geographical zoning was dismissed as a useful tool in its pure geographical form, it would appear that two different zones have been identified inadvertently. There would appear to be fundamental spatial differences between *Regiones* 6 and 7 that could be explained by the fact that land rents in the centre would have been higher than those elsewhere in the city. This might be used to explain the level of street activity in this area. However, I would suggest an alternative explanation, which does not exclude the concept of economic zoning, in terms of centre and periphery.[3] The area to the east of the forum (*Regio 7*) forms a central core that integrates the rest of the system. The fact that it does not rely upon orthogonal planning may be its greatest strength. Indeed, its role as an integrating core may be dependent upon its irregularity. Other areas that are orthogonally planned (for example *Regio* 9.1–4) do not appear capable of taking on such a role. The combination of an irregular plan and centrality greatly increases the inhabitant–inhabitant interface within this region. Other areas of Pompeii do not reflect this relationship to the same degree, because of their position and their regular orthogonal plan.

The question of what was generating this pattern needs to be answered. The street pattern itself appears to have been partially determinate; also, the role of position within that street pattern has been addressed. The role of the internal structuring of *insula* blocks would appear to have been another factor. *Regiones* 6 and 7 were selected as areas in which the internal pattern of the *insula* blocks seemed to play a role in the organisation of external space.

The role of the *atrium* house type as indicated by the *fauces* might have had a determining role in the subdivision of *insula* blocks. This proposition was tested in the two study regions, *Regiones* 6 and 7, by plotting the number of *fauces* on each side of each *insula* (Map 7.4). From Map 7.4 it would appear that the variation in the number of *fauces* occurring was not

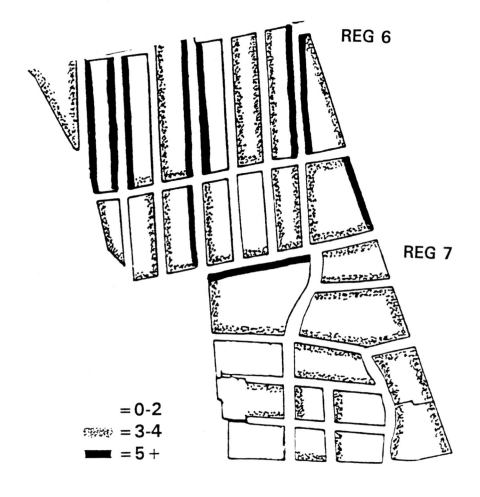

REG 6

REG 7

= 0-2
= 3-4
= 5 +

Map 7.4 The number of *fauces*

large enough to support the conclusion that this was a primary factor in the structuring of external space. It was from such inconclusive data that it was decided that it was necessary to increase the resolution of study. The level that was adopted retained the street as the larger unit of study, but viewed the spatial configurations within the *insula* blocks as though they were seen by a stranger or a visitor. That is, the study looks at the spatial structures of houses adjoining the streets from the point of view of a person in the street, rather than from that of the inhabitant or owner of the house. Each individual structure within a street was drawn in a morphic language of space (for a full account of the methodology see Hillier and Hanson 1984). This morphic language was made up of two components: dots and lines. The dots signify the existence of rooms, spaces or corridors and the lines represent the connections between the rooms, spaces or corridors. For example, in Figure 7.1, the morphic language of the House of the Vettii is set out. This methodology defines the spaces in a structure and emphasises the relationship between spaces. Therefore, an emphasis is placed upon the spaces or voids, rather than solids or walls, which are emphasised in the plans of houses. Once the houses have been converted into this morphic language, they can be analysed using the methods of Hillier and Hanson (1984). The number of spaces within a structure can be established: in our example, there are twenty-nine. These spaces can be seen to have varied in their depth from the street. For example, the *fauces* is the shallowest point, whereas the peristyle tends to be one of deeper spaces. To account for this variation the mean depth of the house was calculated. In our example, we find that the House of the Vettii has a mean depth of 3.6. This accounts for the overall position of the spaces in a house in relationship to the street. However, to account fully for the degree of integration or separation of a house from the street, it is necessary to utilise an equation devised for this purpose by Hillier and Hanson (1984: 147–55):

$$RA = \frac{2(MD - 1)}{K - 2}$$

where

RA = Relative Asymmetry
MD = Mean Depth
K = Number of Spaces.

This equation results in the measurement of Relative Asymmetry, which summarises the arrangement of the house in numerical form. The results of this equation vary from 0.00 to 1.00. In our example of the House of the Vettii:

$$RA = \frac{2(MD - 1)}{K - 2}$$

$$RA = \frac{2(3.6 - 1)}{29 - 2}$$

$$RA = 0.19.$$

Therefore the House of the Vettii has a Relative Asymmetry of 0.19, which can be compared with measurements of Relative Asymmetry in other houses. The figure of 0.19 suggests that the House of the Vettii is strongly integrated into the street structure. The main reason for this is the depth of the house in relationship to the number of spaces contained in the house. The usefulness of this method lies in its ability to examine and compare the variation in the structure of space that does not appear on the plans of houses.

However, our concern is not so much with the houses themselves, but with the variation in settlement types in relationship to the street structure of the city. Therefore, in each street the Mean Depth, the Number of Spaces and the Relative Asymmetry were calculated for each structure. Then the mean of these values was used as a description of the amount of integration or separation between any one street and its adjoining *insulae*. The number of structures that formed distributive units was also noted. For example, the House of the Vettii can be entered from Vicolo dei Vettii and Vicolo di Mercurio, so that it forms a distributive unit between two streets.

This process produced an array of data for the streets in the two study regions. The data highlighted the major differences and similarities between *Regiones* 6 and 7. The range of the Mean Depth in *Regio* 7 was from 1.0 to 2.4; whereas in *Regio* 6 it varied from 1.8 to 3.3. The mean number of spaces within buildings in a street varied from 5 to 11 in *Regio* 7, whereas in *Regio* 6 it was in the range of 5 to 15. The similarity between these figures is caused partly by the inclusion of the through-route, Via delle Terme and Via della Fortuna, in the *Regio* 6 sample. If these two streets are excluded from the sample the range is markedly higher, 12 to 15. Therefore, the properties in *Regio* 6 were considerably larger than those in *Regio* 7. We may also assume that as a result there were probably fewer properties in *Regio* 6. This might generate the pattern of doorway and message occurrence that was observed in Chapter 6. This would also imply that fewer people would have been encountered in *Regio* 6 than in *Regio* 7. Some of the properties in both *regiones* were defined as not having depth and were fully integrated with the street. Generally, in *Regio* 7 there were more properties in each street that lacked depth than properties with depth. In *Regio* 6, excluding Via della Fortuna and Via delle Terme, the majority of streets had more properties with depth than without. These observations need to be borne in mind in the following discussion of Relative Asymmetry. This was a measure of integration of properties with the street that can vary between 0.00 and 1.0. The

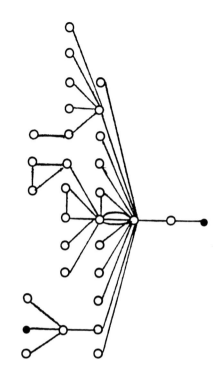

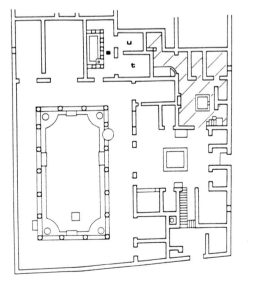

Figure 7.1 The House of the Vettii in plan and as a morphic language

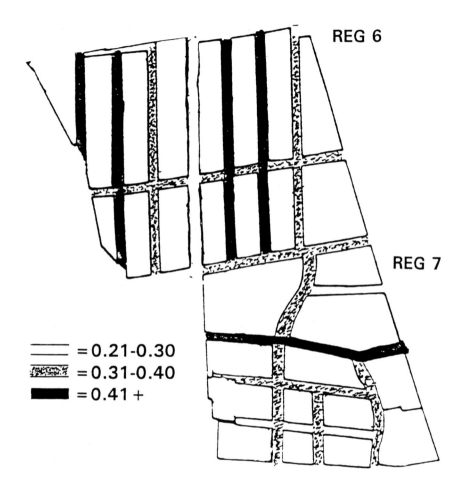

REG 6

REG 7

= 0.21-0.30
= 0.31-0.40
= 0.41 +

Map 7.5 Relative Asymmetry

Table 7.1 Summary of data for *Regio* 7

	Mean values			With depth	Without depth
Street	MD	SP	RA		
Augustali	2.0	6	0.49	33%	67%
Maschera	2.3	9	0.39	45%	55%
Scheletri	2.1	9	0.29	32%	68%
Balcone Pensile	2.4	9	0.39	37%	63%
Eumachia	1.8	5	0.34	26%	74%
Lupanare	1.8	6	0.34	38%	62%
Panettiere	2.2	11	0.24	50%	50%
Storto	1.8	7	0.33	45%	55%

Table 7.2 Summary of data for *Regio* 6

	Mean values			With depth	Without depth
Street	MD	SP	RA		
Mercurio (vicolo)	2.9	13	0.37	79%	21%
Fullonica	3.2	15	0.38	94%	6%
Mercurio (via)	2.7	15	0.28	67%	33%
Fortuna	2.1	8	0.37	38%	62%
Fauno	3.3	14	0.41	75%	25%
Labirinto	2.9	12	0.43	89%	11%
Vettii	2.7	15	0.39	81%	19%
Terme	1.8	5	0.40	37%	63%
Modesto	3.1	12	0.45	83%	17%
Narciso	3.1	13	0.50	86%	14%

lower the figure of Relative Asymmetry, the greater the integration of the building with the street. However, if the figure rises above 1 or cannot be calculated because of its lack of spaces or depth, it is said to be without depth and fully integrated with the street. The range of mean Relative Asymmetry was remarkably similar, from 0.24 to 0.49 in *Regio* 7 and from 0.28 to 0.50 in *Regio* 6. The highest figure for *Regio* 7 occurred in Via degli Augustali, whilst the lowest figure for *Regio* 6 occurred in Via di Mercurio. Both of these streets have high occurrences of doorways, but the relationship between the buildings and the street is completely different, as indicated by the figures for Relative Asymmetry. The reason for such a variation is that in both streets there were good reasons for siting property there, in competition with other property, but the way and the reasons for siting it there were rather different. In Via degli Augustali the larger houses insulated themselves from the street. The low figure of Relative Asymmetry for Via di Mercurio marks a desire to integrate the property with the street. This

Plate 7.3 View from the *fauces* through *atrium* into the peristyle (6.8.23)

should come as no surprise, because the visual narrative from the outside would have revealed the structure of space through to the peristyle at the rear. The reason that there was a high occurrence of doorways in this area is not that street activity was high, but rather that those requiring formality and separation from the street wanted to live in this street within easy reach of the forum.

In other streets the range of Relative Asymmetry was not significantly different (see Map 7.5). The similarity can be accounted for. The *atrium* house would appear to have two different entrances: the formal one through the *fauces*, and an informal rear entrance. The rear entrance of these houses would appear to have been separated from the street, whereas the formal entrance was integrated with it. Another reason for this apparent similarity is inherent in the way the data are presented. Only those properties that had depth could have the level of their integration measured. This means that all those properties without depth are excluded from the analysis of Relative Asymmetry. Therefore, the similarity between the figures for *Regiones* 6 and 7 points not to a similarity between the two areas of study, but rather to a similarity of property type in the two study areas. The fact that there is a greater amount of property without depth in *Regio* 7 than with depth and vice versa in *Regio* 6 points to the major differences between the two areas. In other words, the larger properties in *Regio* 7 have a greater tendency to be spatially separated from the street, whereas those in *Regio* 6 have a greater tendency to be formally separated from it.

The occurrence of similar property types in two structurally different areas of the city is most illuminating. In *Regio* 7, properties separated from the street to the same degree as in *Regio* 6 exist alongside properties that lack depth and are integrated with the street. This suggests that a hierarchy of space or economic zoning of space does not exist in *Regio* 7. Equally, in *Regio* 6 there does not appear to be a hierarchy of space or separation of groups, although it must be stated that there is conscious separation of property from the street.

Some general factors which produced the patterns of doorway occurrences do emerge from this study of Pompeii. Where the mean number of spaces is high, doorway occurrences tend to be low. Where doorway occurrences are high, Mean Depth tends to be low. Where doorway occurrences are high, the percentage of structures without depth is greater than the percentage of structures with depth. Where doorway occurrences are low, Mean Depth tends to be high. Where doorway occurrences are low, the percentage of structures with depth is greater than the percentage of structures without. It is this series of inverse relationships that would appear to be generating the spatial pattern of doorway occurrences. This would appear to be the spatial logic that generates patterns in Pompeii; it is related to the amount of activity and the density of settlement in an area. These two factors highlight *Regio* 7 as an area of intense activity not replicated in other areas of the city, where the density of the use of the urban fabric is not as great. In these areas, the urban fabric could have been designed to isolate a property from the street. This can only be done because the pressure upon space is not great. However, in *Regio* 7, the pressure upon the usage of the street frontage prohibited the isolation of property from the street.

8

THE TEMPORAL LOGIC
OF SPACE

This chapter sets out to define spatial activities in a temporal context. It utilises the literary sources to define the availability of activities. These literary sources emphasise the elite activities rather than a universal temporal pattern of activity. However, it would appear that the space–time patterning of elite activity structured the use of space in the Roman city.

The Lund school of urban geographers developed a method for understanding human activity in both a temporal and a spatial context (Herbert and Thomas 1982: 362; Carlstein 1982: 38–64; Soja 1989; Giddens 1984; Harvey 1988). The underlying assumption of all studies of space in a temporal context is that each individual has a pattern of movement, which centres around the workplace, home, shopping and recreation. This arrangement of movement reflects personal preferences for certain types of activity, their spatial location, and the relative distribution and availability of these activities. Some activities have a fixed time and place, for example school. The movement to and from regular activities creates a pattern, which is dependent upon the availability of these activities in time and space (Herbert and Thomas 1982: 363). This regular pattern of availability creates a rhythmic pattern of movement, which in turn orders the urban environment.

Significantly, it would appear that the temporal availability of any one activity is not independent of the temporal availability of other activities. In fact, they form 'a highly integrated and coordinated structure within which individual life patterns must be contained' (Herbert and Thomas 1982: 365).

Much of the literary evidence concerns the city of Rome. Therefore, in this chapter, I seek to establish first that time was an important parameter in the use of the city. Then I compare this structure with those of the countryside and other urban settlements outside Rome. Finally, I shall propose a temporal structure for the use of space in Pompeii.

Before we can begin to study the space–time solidarities of the Roman city, we need to understand the ancient conception and comprehension of time. It has been observed by modern historians that the Industrial Revolution altered people's conception of time from task time to clock time (Thompson 1967; see also the debate between Harrison 1986 and Landes

1987). Other variations in the conception of time can occur. For example, in a seaport time is dominated by tides (Thompson 1967: 60). Another factor is biological time, measured by eating and sleeping. There is also psychological time, associated with the amount of time spent on any one activity (Herbert and Thomas 1982: 365). Only by understanding the Roman concept and measurement of time can we begin to set up a model of space–time solidarities.

The Roman concept of time was dominated by a measurement of daylight and darkness. The primary division was between day and night (Gell. 3.2.9; Colum. 10.42; an equinox was naturally a time of equal day and night). Each day and each night were divided into twelve hours. The length of an hour varied seasonally (Ovid, *Met.* 4.199, Pont. 2.10.38; Lucan 10.218. The hour was not the sixty-minute hour of today). Balsdon (1969: 18) gives the variation of daylight in modern hours: the longest day was from 04.30 to 19.30 and the shortest day was from 07.30 to 16.30. Therefore, the length of a Roman hour would vary from summer to winter. At the winter solstice the Roman hour would have been forty-five minutes long, whereas at the summer solstice it would have been seventy-five minutes long. The summer solstice was six hours longer than the winter solstice. Figure 8.1 illustrates this variation in the day: the greatest differences appear at the extremities of the day; the central hours such as the sixth and, in particular, the seventh did not have such a wide variation. Significantly, the seventh hour began at the same point in real time summer and winter. This was essential, because it was at the seventh hour that many activities recommenced after an hour of rest. The seasonal variation of daylight and, therefore, the length of the hours was understood, but there was no measurement of such a concept.

However, there were intricate devices for measuring time. These included accurate sundials and water clocks, which allowed for the measurement of time on cloudy days (see Gibbs 1976 on sundials; Plin., *N.H.* 7.212–15 on water clocks). Slaves were also employed to inform people of the time (Juv. 10.216). Moreover, there was an understanding of time zones (Plin., *N.H.* 6.214 divides the world into time zones). This knowledge led to the development of sundials for travellers, which were adjustable according to the latitude people had reached (Plin., *N.H.* 2.182). The measurement of time varied from place to place, and so sundials were set up in public places in cities to tell travellers the local time as well (Vitr. 9.8). Pliny also noted (*N.H.* 18.133, 18.252) that in the country-side the time could be told according to the diurnal movement of the lupin. The interest in the measurement of time and the availability of timepieces in cities suggest that there was an important temporal dimension to public life and the use of space. This appreciation of time allowed for the arrangement of meetings at a certain hour of the day (Cic., *Quinct.* 25, Verr. 2.2.91; Ovid, *Ars* 2.223; Sen., *Benef.* 1.23). In terms of

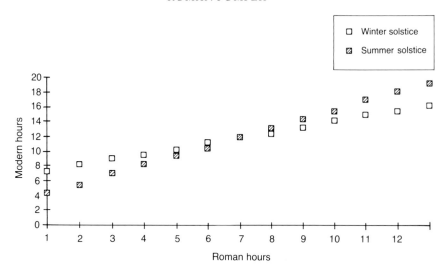

Figure 8.1 Variation in Roman time

documentation, someone's life could be measured in years, months, days and finally hours (see, e.g., *CIL* 6.2931). Thus, time was accurately measured to the hour.

Within this structure of time, certain activities were defined and available at set times in the day. In Figure 8.2, the diurnal availability of activities at Rome is set out. Each activity will be examined in turn to present the temporal logic that structured the use of the city.

Public business, such as the meeting of the senate, could take place at any hour during daylight (Gell. 14.7.8). However, it should be remembered that prior to any public event the auspices needed to be observed. This would have required daylight. If the omens were bad, an activity could have been delayed (see, e.g., Suet., *Nero* 8: on the announcement of Claudius' death, Nero did not go to the praetorian camp until the seventh or eighth hour, because there were bad omens). However, once public business was under way it could continue all day.

The baths appear to have been available from the sixth hour until at least the eleventh (Vitr. 10.1: Suet., *Dom.* 16.2; Juv. 11.205; Cic., *Att.* 13.52; Vitr. 5.10; Nielsen 1990: 112–38; Balsdon 1969: 28–9). In our sources bathing seems to have been preferred from the sixth to the eighth hours. Martial notes that the baths were at their hottest at the sixth hour until about the eighth hour, when they began to cool down (Mart. 10.48.3).

The opening times of the temple of Isis emulated this diurnal structure. The temple opened at the first hour and closed at the eighth (Apul., *Met.* 11.20; Mart. 10.48.3), the eighth hour being the end of the public day. This might indicate a diurnal structure from the first to the eighth hour for the availability of religious worship (Solmsen 1979: 69–70 and 92).

The *salutatio* began at dawn (Hor., *Ep.* 2.1.104; Mart. 3.36, 10.70). The client in Rome might have made a long journey to visit his patron, perhaps more than two miles (Mart. 2.5). The *salutatio* would have lasted until the end of the second hour (Mart. 4.8). After the *salutatio*, the client might have followed his patron until the tenth hour (Mart. 3.36.5, 10.70). The writer of the *Commentarium Petitionis* instructed Cicero to go down to the forum at regular times, so that people knew when he was going and they could easily follow him (Comm. Pet. 34, 36). This would suggest that time was widely observed by Cicero's followers and the population of the city in general. Therefore, the movement of clients to the *salutatio* and the regular movement of a patron followed by his clients to the forum created a spatial order that was temporally set to cause a senator's arrival in the forum, accompanied by some clients, by the third hour.

The courts were in session from the third hour in the forum (Mart. 4.8). The sessions could be lengthy: for example, at Milo's trial in 56 BC Pompey

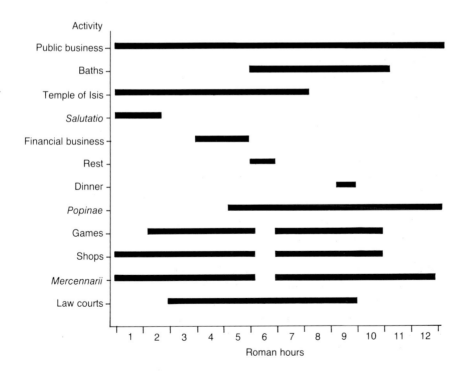

Figure 8.2 The availability of activities

125

spoke until the sixth hour, and Clodius was still speaking at the ninth hour, when the meeting erupted in violence (Cic., *Q.F.* 2.3.2). If his patron was in court, a client would expect to be engaged until the tenth hour (Mart. 10.70; Hor., *Epist.* 1.7.46). However, the court might be adjourned after only an hour (Mart. 8.67.1). The potential availability of court activity was between the third and tenth hours.

The fourth and fifth hours were associated with business and financial transactions (Mart. 4.8), which were expected to be completed by the sixth hour (Plu., *Q.R.* 84). The sixth hour was often associated with rest and relaxation (Mart. 4.8; Plin., *Ep.* 3.5, 9.44.2; Cels. 1.2.5; Cic., *De Orat.* 3.17). A similar siesta period can be seen in the countryside. In summer, animals would have been unyoked and flocks would be driven into the shade (Plin., *N.H.* 18.330; Mart. 3.67). Varro advised that a shelter should be erected for threshers for relaxation at the sixth hour (Varro, *R.R.*1.51.2). There would appear to be some seasonal variation. Pliny the Younger (*Ep.* 9.44.2) had a siesta at the sixth hour in the summer, but not in the winter. In July 45 BC Cicero rested for three hours at Lanuvium on his way to Astura (Cic., *Att.* 13.34). It seems likely that much activity ceased at the sixth hour in summer for a siesta. This time coincided with the time when the baths were at their hottest: the availability of the baths was designed to coincide with this rest period at midday.

Ammianus Marcellinus noted (23.6.77) that the Persians had no fixed time for eating and that their meal times were governed by their biological clock, rather than the sundial. From this remark, it is clear that the Roman conception of time structured eating habits. The hour for dinner was the ninth; dinner might have been followed by some form of entertainment, for example poetry (Mart. 4.8).

It appears that the *popinae* were open by the fourth hour. Ampelius, city prefect in AD 371–2, gave orders that no *taberna vinaria* should open before the fourth hour. As we have seen in Chapter 5, the elite tended not to eat in public, and the *popinae* and *tabernae* were places that they did not enter (Cic., *Pis.* 13, Quinct. 6.3.63). The *popinae* might stay open all night (Juv. 8.158; Amm. Marc. 14.6.25). However, this does not imply that all *popinae* remained open, but rather that the activity of going to a *popina* was available throughout the night and most of the day.

The games began early in the morning, the crowd arriving at dawn or shortly afterwards (Suet., *Claud.* 34.2). There was a break at the sixth hour, for about an hour (Suet., *Claud.* 34.2; Dio 37.46.4). However, at *munera*, more humiliating killings continued during this hour (Suet., *Claud.* 34.2; Tert., *Apol.* 15.5; Coleman 1990). It is possible to determine the start of the games more precisely. Horace states that a theatre play would be four hours long (Hor., *Epist.* 2.1.189). If there was a break at the sixth hour, it would be necessary to begin the play at the second hour. The end of the games in the evening can also be deduced. The games would begin again at the seventh hour and continue for four hours until the eleventh hour.

The activity of workshops and shops began early in the morning. Bakeries were open before dawn and workshops would have been open all day (Mart. 12.57). Shops appear to have opened certainly by the second hour (Plin., *N.H.* 7.182), and some stayed open until the evening, even up to the eleventh hour (Petr., *Sat.* 12; Aug., *Conf.* 3.7.13; Mart. 9.59; Hor., *Sat.* 1.6.113). However, this does not mean that all shops were open from dawn to the eleventh hour. Shops tend to be responsive to other areas of activity and open and close accordingly. For example, it is certain that the shops near the baths were open at times of activity in the baths (Sen., *Ep.* 56.1–2). At periods of inactivity in the baths, these shops might have closed.

The hired labourer (*mercennarius*) would have worked all day and was hired by the day for a set rate (Hor., *Ep.* 1.1.20; Matt. 20; see also Treggiari 1980: 51). In our sources, the *mercennarius* was associated particularly with various harvests. These naturally occurred in the longer summer days (Varro, *R.R.* 1.17). Night work was also known (Crook 1967: 196), and was made possible by artificial light. Working during the night may well have been normal in winter (Colum. 11.29.1).

In total this information, as presented in Figure 8.2, represents the temporal availability of activities in the city and surrounding countryside. Some of the activities follow on from one another. For example, a member of the elite began his day with the *salutatio*. Then he left his house and went to the forum to take part in a meeting of the senate, a court case or other public business. These activities could keep the senator or *eques* away from his house until maybe the tenth hour, a factor which has important implications for the social structure of the households of the elite. For most of the day, the male members of the household were outside the house. Although there was no structural division of female and male space in the house (Wallace-Hadrill 1988: 50–2), there was a temporal division of this space. If the male member of the household was out from the second to the eighth or ninth hours, for half the day the house was a female space. The space was male-dominated at the *salutatio* and at dinner at the ninth hour. Therefore, the beginning and end of the day were male-dominated, whereas the central portion of the day was female-controlled. This structural division emphasises male activity outside the home, and even when male activity occurred in the home, it reflected the male world of politics. In contrast, female activity was concentrated in the house and was spatially constrained. This division would produce completely different patterns of encounter for each gender. The male use of the household reflected a man's external self, as a politician. At the same time the household emphasised the external role of the male head of the household to visitors. The interior embodies the self and enhances the representation of the self at a global or city-wide level (Hillier and Hanson 1984: 260). The female self would

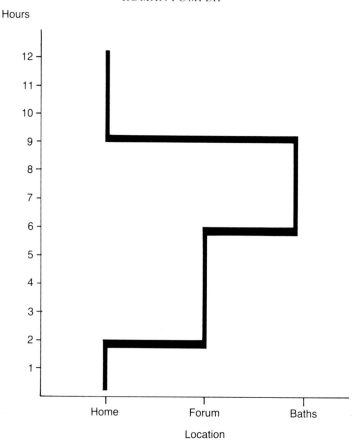

Figure 8.3 The location of the elite in space and time

seem not to have been represented, because it was subjugated to the external self of the *paterfamilias*. The female self was restricted in expression to the hours when the male member of the household was away for most of the day. For the elite, the spatial encounter patterns were divided by gender.[1]

To return to the male member of the elite in the forum, his day would have been over by the sixth hour if he was not involved in public business for longer. This was the time when the baths were at their hottest (Mart. 10.48.3). If a person's leisure or *otium* commenced at the sixth hour, they could use the baths at their hottest. It is apparent that the owner of a shop or *popina*, and the *mercennarii* could not utilise the baths at this point in the day, because of the need to attend to their work or business. Thus, the baths were utilised primarily by the elite between the sixth and eighth hours, when they were hot. It might be the case that the majority of the population did not experience hot baths, if they bathed after the tenth hour or later. For the elite, the bath was accompanied by exercise. Subsequently, they returned home or were invited to dine elsewhere at the ninth hour.

The activities of the elite structured city space. Their pattern of movement established a routine. In the morning, they received their clients at their house; from there they went to the forum accompanied by their clients, from the forum they went to the baths, and finally they returned home. The temporal aspect of this routine articulates city space. Between the second and third hours the elite migrated to the forum, from all parts of the city. At the sixth hour, they went to the baths, unless public business delayed them, in which case they would go to the baths later, but before the tenth hour. Given the emphasis upon display, it would seem likely that the elite need not have bathed locally near their homes, but would enjoy the display of walking to baths further away. For example, the baths on the Campus Martius were not in a residential locality. At the ninth hour, there would have been a migration back to their houses for dinner. This regular pattern meant that the elite were seen at a certain time and place each day. The elite were mobile and visible outside their localities.

In contrast, the rest of the population of Rome would not have been as mobile. The separation of work and leisure has been shown to be less pronounced in pre-industrial societies (Thompson 1967: 59). Furthermore, the separation of workplace and residence was not strongly emphasised. Life was centred upon the home, in which work was carried out. Female and male space were not divided temporally or physically (but *CIL* 2.5181 suggests that male and female times for bathing could be different). Unlike the elite, the majority of the population led their lives within the locality of the home.

It was the elite and their clients who were mobile within the city. This suggests that there were at least two sets of time operating (for the operation of contradictory sets of time see Salas 1966; Le Goff 1960): the structured day of the elite that took them away from their place of residence, and the unstructured day of the rest of the population, which was centred upon their place of residence.

The activity pattern of the elite was not universally adhered to. Horace suggested that his life was better than a senator's. His reasoning was simple: he did not have to get up early; he could lie in bed until the fourth hour, then get up and go for a walk. He might write or read something. At the sixth hour, he would go to the baths; then he would return home to his meal and idle the day away (Hor., *Sat.* 1.6.122). This alternative time scheme coincided with the elite's schedule at the baths and at dinner. This would give Horace the chance to encounter patrons from elite families.

It would appear that time in the countryside was constructed differently. We have a limited amount of evidence for elite time sequences in the countryside. Pliny (*Ep.* 9.36) kept to a routine when he stayed at his Tuscan villa. At the first hour he would get up; he then contemplated in the dark and called his secretary in order to dictate his thoughts. At the fourth or fifth hour, he would go outside on to the terrace and continue dictating, then he walked and read aloud or was read to by a slave. In summer, he would take a siesta at the sixth hour (*Ep*. 9.40.2); afterwards, he would walk and exercise. He then took his bath at the eighth hour and at the ninth hour had dinner with his wife and a few friends, after which they listened to a musician. Finally, he took a walk with his household slaves.[2] This routine resembles city time: rest at the sixth hour, baths at the eighth hour and dinner at the ninth hour. However, the rest of the day remained unstructured, like Horace's day. The gender division of city time is also apparent. Contact between Pliny and his wife was only mentioned at dinner and afterwards. Country time for the elite resembled city time, except that their day was given over to *otium* and not restricted by the need to utilise the forum and transact public business.

The retired senator Spurrina had a different temporal pattern at his villa in the country (Plin., *Ep*. 3.1.8). He spent the first part of the morning in bed, and got up at the second hour. His first activity was a walk, whilst being read to. He then went for a drive in his chariot with his wife; after they had travelled seven miles, they walked for about a mile, and when they returned home, he studied and wrote. At the eighth hour in summer, the ninth in winter, he took his bath, and exercised by throwing a ball. Spurrina and his wife ate at the ninth hour, and at the tenth hour they watched a comedy. Again the day was structured, as in the city, around bathing and dining. The temporal gender separation is not as great. Also, visitors, when they appeared, were controlled and restricted to the dinner hour or, if privileged, they stayed for a few days.

This rural pattern, which excluded visitors, did not exist in the towns of Italy outside Rome. Cicero visited Formiae in April 59 BC (Cic., *Att*. 2.14.2), and his activity pattern was quite different from that at Rome or the country villa. Cicero, as an ex-consul and senator, was in effect a celebrity to be seen, and in the morning many people visited him. He states that he was detained till the fourth hour, and even after that the *vulgus* continued to come. Indeed, it would appear that a senator spent his time meeting people in the towns of Italy: the arrival of a senator would disrupt the normal space–time patterning in the town.[3]

Outside Rome, a senator's space–time allocation to activities was quite different. In the towns of Italy, a greater amount of time was spent meeting people; less in a rural setting. This structure of time allocation would have affected the use of space, and the organisation of that space.

The pattern of elite space–time at Rome was coordinated around the rituals of decision making in the senate, the assembly and the law courts. Similarly, the lives of the elite were dominated by the rituals associated with their role in decision making. The space–time pattern is different in the country. The emphasis in the countryside upon bathing and eating at a set hour should be seen as separate and universal, whether in town or country. For the rest of the population, including the female elite, the space–time pattern was localised in city and country, with a concentration of activity near the place of residence.

Can we apply this temporal framework to Pompeii? The elite in both Rome and Pompeii devoted a considerable amount of their time to public business and political decision making in the forum. The emphasis on the rituals of reception and dining in the houses of Pompeii has been stressed by a number of scholars (Wallace-Hadrill 1988; Clarke 1991). In many ways, the lives of the elite at Pompeii mirrored the lives of the elite at Rome. The major differences were in size and scale in the lives of the urban population in the two cities, rather than any major dissimilarities in the underlying structure of urban life. The temporal framework outlined above may well have been standard for most cities in Italy, which would suggest that such a temporal sequence can be applied to the spatial structure of Pompeii.

The houses of the Pompeian elite were in no way separate from those of the less privileged; they did not cluster round the forum, baths, temples or other prestigious buildings. However, there might be a logic behind the location of an elite household. This logic might not be spatial but, rather, a temporal arrangement of the elite's lifestyle. By using the example of M. Obellius Firmus, one of Caecilius Jucundus' witnesses, who had held the offices of aedile and *duumvir*, we can begin to understand the temporal dynamic that structured urban life (Jongman 1988: 207–30). At dawn, clients probably gathered at Obellius Firmus' house (9.14.4) in Via di Nola, from where they departed at the end of the second hour for the forum in procession. Presumably, Obellius Firmus spent time in the forum until the sixth hour, when he might have departed with his clients to the baths. After spending time at the baths, he returned home for dinner at the ninth hour. His life would have been structured around the need to be at a certain place at a certain time each day. A key part of elite display was the movement through the city with an entourage of clients. To fulfil this need, the place of residence needed to be a short distance from the forum; the baths needed to be a short distance from the forum and the place of residence, to create the possibility of people going about their daily lives seeing the passage of a member of the elite through the city. Also, for much of the day members of the elite would have been out of the house. This would cause a gender division of space in time. In the first two hours of the day the house would have been utilised by Obellius Firmus for the purpose of receiving clients. At the end of the second hour until just before the ninth hour it would be dominated by the activities of the household without the adult male presence of the *paterfamilias*. At the ninth hour, the house would revert to the role of receiving guests and emphasising the position of the *paterfamilias* in Pompeian society. Therefore, in the Pompeian house, gender divisions which are spatially indistinct were emphasised temporally. It is such a temporal logic of elite activity that locates the public buildings and, in particular, the public baths. Also, the need for the elite's place of residence to have been separate from the place of social activity distributed the elite throughout the city, rather than concentrating them in any one area.

However, for the majority of the population such a temporal structure did not apply. The *mercennarius* worked from dawn to dusk with a break at the sixth hour (Hor., *Ep.* 1.1.20; Matt. 20; Treggiari 1980; Varro, *R.R.* 1.17), the shops opened from dawn until the eleventh hour (Plin., *N.H.* 7.182) and the *popinae* opened from the fourth hour and might not close until late into the night (Cic., *Pis.* 13, Quinct. 6.3.63; Juv. 8.158; Amm. Marc. 14.6.25). Thus for the rest of the population, such temporal concerns were less relevant, and it was the nature of the street structure that organised their lives spatially. For the *mercennarius*, the place of work was often his place of residence. The break for an hour at midday for rest would have punctuated the day. It should also be recognised that the pre-industrial concepts of time associated with work were far more task-orientated than our own conception of work, associated with a set number of hours per day (Thompson 1967). The day of the *mercennarius* would have been orientated and punctuated by the arrival of customers and deliveries, rather than the ritualised time sequences of the elite, which were orientated towards the reception of clients, public business, bathing and dining at set times each day.

By understanding the temporal sequences of the elite, we can account for the dispersal pattern of elite houses, which needed to be separate from one another to facilitate separate processions of clients to the forum during the first and second hours. Also, the separation of the forum from the baths was important to allow further processions of the elite and their clients later in the day. Finally, the baths were located at a distance from the homes of the elite because there was a final procession from the baths home. In this context, zoning was neither desirable nor possible without restructuring the nature of elite display.

9

URBANISM
IN ROMAN ITALY

It has been repeatedly argued in the preceding chapters that models such as the 'consumer city' or 'service city' do not provide a full explanation of the Roman city. This chapter seeks to view the Pompeian evidence in the wider context of Roman urbanism, and to define the nature of the Roman city. Models such as the 'consumer city' rely upon the analysis of economic production. Although the city is seen as the consumer of produce from the countryside, the economic nature of consumption is never explained. Equally, the opposition of city and countryside, such a prominent aspect of these models, may not be as relevant in pre-capitalist societies (Giddens 1981: 117). However, we should not focus solely upon the economic aspect of the Roman city. David Harvey (1988: 22) sums up the problem: 'The city is manifestly a complicated thing. Part of the difficulty we experience in dealing with it can be attributed to this inherent complexity. But our problems can also be attributed to our failure to conceptualise the situation correctly.' The models used by ancient historians have oversimplified the Roman city. These models tend to be based upon Weber's explanation of the evolution of the Western city. Weber's intention was to account for the formation of the capitalist city, rather than to explain the ancient city. In any case, Weber's work has been strongly criticised by urban theorists (e.g. Saunders 1986: 28–38). The adoption of Weber's ideal types of city by ancient history was never problematised. The debate around the consumer-city model was based upon agreement or disagreement with the propositions of Moses Finley's argument, and about whether that argument was substantiated by the ancient evidence. No theoretical debate about the nature of urbanism was conducted. Twenty years on, the consumer city is viewed as the best model we have, but most authors express their dissatisfaction with it (e.g. Whittaker 1990). There are other models available. These tend to be put forward by urban theorists working on the city in the modern world. However, some of their models can be applied to urbanism, capitalist or non-capitalist.

An alternative to Weber's analysis has been presented by David Harvey (1988; for a critique see Deutsche 1991; Massey 1991; Wolff 1992, to be read with Smith 1992). This should not be seen as a rejection of Weber's work but, rather, as a more sophisticated analysis of the relationship between cities and surplus. Surplus in this context is seen as being social and/or economic. Harvey (1988: 238–40) makes a series of propositions:

1 Cities are built forms created by the mobilisation and geographic concentration of significant quantities of a socially defined surplus product.
2 Urbanism represents a pattern of individual activity which forms a mode of economic and social integration which mobilises and concentrates a socially defined surplus product.
3 A surplus product of a social nature is produced by all societies, and it is always possible to create more of it. The concept of this surplus may change as conditions of consumption, production and distribution change.
4 Urbanism is more likely to occur in the following circumstances: (a) there is a large total population; (b) this population is settled and immobile; (c) there is a relatively high density of population; (d) there is potential for high productivity; (e) there is easy communication and access.
5 The mobilisation and concentration of a social surplus in cities on a permanent basis implies that the circumstances in (4) existed.
6 Urbanism necessarily arises with the emergence of a market mode of economic integration and its associated social stratification.
7 Urbanism can assume a variety of forms depending upon the particular function of the urban centre with respect to the total pattern of circulation of the socially defined social product.
8 There need not be a direct relationship between urbanism and economic growth. Urbanism is very much a social product.
9 Urbanism depends upon the geographic concentration of a social surplus. If there is no concentration of this surplus, urbanism does not occur.

Underlying all these propositions is the assumption that urbanism may be regarded as a particular form or patterning of social processes. Therefore, the city is very much a product of its society (Harvey 1988:196). However, it is a surplus product, because the existence of a city is not a necessity to fulfil the minimum calorific requirements of a population. In Roman Italy, the social surplus was expressed via urbanism. Roman urbanism was a social form, or a way of life distinct from that of the countryside or of the barbarians outside the Roman world. It would appear that the realisation of the social surplus in the form known as urbanism was the dominant mode of social production and reproduction in the Roman Empire. However, it needs to be recognised that the city as a social product was not realised overnight. The Roman city seen at any given date was the result of earlier accumulation and production. Furthermore, the Roman city and urbanism coincided with the need for

Roman society to remain stable and reproduce itself. In many ways, the city in Roman Italy was the mode of production of Roman society: it was the centre of power, the centre of privilege, the centre of culture and the centre of knowledge (Harvey 1988: 203). Therefore, in Roman Italy, the social surplus was concentrated at one point in space, i.e. in the city (Harvey 1988: 226).

Urbanism needs to be seen as a social product in time and space. It goes without saying that a city is a projection of society upon space. This is an elementary but at the same time crucial concept (Castells 1977: 115). The nature, and seeming uniformity, of Roman urbanism would have allowed anyone arriving for the first time in a city such as Pompeii to find their way to the forum, the centre of power. In this, they would have been aided by their own perception of the city and experiences of other cities (Lefebvre 1991: 162). Moreover, they would have been aided by a series of signs and an ability to comprehend them (Foucault 1984a). For example, the forum would have been found by observing the position of the tallest temple, and following the wider streets in its general direction. There would also have been subtler signs, such as the degree to which street fronts were used for commercial purposes or the number of people in the street. The stranger would also categorise people from their appearance and gestures. In doing so, the stranger would not enquire to learn more about them, but categorise them according to a series of signs (Raban 1974; Harvey 1990: 3–7). For example, the prostitute would have been immediately categorised according to her dress. This is an extreme example: others would have been perceived according to more subtle signs. The stranger, in fact, would have re-created the city visited according to their own personal preconceptions of what they saw and had experienced.

This accounts for how the city was viewed, but what was the process that produced the urban form familiar to us from Pompeii? The urban fabric of Pompeii was the result of a process of accumulation. Urban history is the history of accumulation in cities. For example, the original layout of Pompeii was gradually transformed as the requirements and priorities of the inhabitants changed. However, no urban space completely vanishes without trace: 'each new addition inherits and reorganises what has gone before'; each period carries its own preconditions into the next period (Lefebvre 1991: 164). In this process we need to recognise that:

> an existing space may outlive its original purpose and its *raison d'être* which determines its forms, functions and structures; it may thus in a sense become vacant and susceptible to being diverted, reappropriated and put to a use quite different from its initial one.
>
> (Lefebvre 1991: 167)

In other words, people use a space in ways that need not coincide with the intentions of its creator. This results in Pompeii in the inscription of

Plate 9.1 Raised pavement outside 8.2.37. Note the difference in materials used

activities and events in the urban fabric over time. Frequently, in Pompeii, we observe the raised pavements outside houses that have been rebuilt at a higher level (see Plate 9.1). The alteration of the internal arrangement of space in the house has an effect upon external space. In this case, the internal space of the house has been transformed, but the external space of the street struggles to remain the same. The roadway has not been altered, but the pavement has been raised to allow access to the new building. This results in a greater separation between the roadway and the pavement. The street structure is different, but continues to reflect its previous reality. In this example, we see how a human intention to alter the structure of a house has caused the unintended consequence (Giddens 1984: 8) that the roadway has become separated from the pavement so that the street cannot be crossed at this point. Therefore, in the Roman city, as in all social situations, we need to remember that there were intentional actions, but unintentional consequences. Furthermore, these intentional actions took place within the existing spatial fabric of the city, which meant that any action to alter that fabric was conditioned by the ideology of those wishing to alter it. In effect, this ideology was strongly influenced by the urban surroundings into which the human actors had been born (Lefebvre 1991: 210).

When we view the public buildings of Pompeii, we begin to see the city and its inhabitants expressing what it is to be a Pompeian. The public buildings concentrated around the forum, the amphitheatre and the theatres are monuments that enshrine the *mentalité* of the ancient world. These monuments offer each individual inhabitant an image of their position in society (Lefebvre 1991: 220). The monuments of the early colony emphasised the defeat and the destruction of the community that had opposed Sulla. The settlement of Roman veterans demanded a new identity for the city, and to accompany that identity a new set of monuments that reflected the new situation. These monuments reflected the colonists' triumph and the original inhabitants' capitulation. The shift in ideology associated with the first emperor was naturally reflected in the monuments of the forum. The inhabitant of Pompeii viewed with awe the shrines associated with the imperial cult, but they could also see the proximity and relevance to their own lives of the imperial family. Once established, temples simply existed (Lefebvre 1991: 250). There was no need to problematise or consider a change for these spaces in the city: they were sacred and viewed as an enduring part of the city's existence. Indeed, the city's existence may have been bound up with the continued maintenance of these sacred spaces. In the forum, there was a close association between the government of the city and these sacred monuments. It should come as no surprise that the position of the emperor was so prominent in the locus of the city's power, the forum. Other public buildings with an emphasis upon ritual, the theatres and the amphitheatre, were also bound up with the emperor's person. For the viewer of the games, their position in society with respect to others was made apparent. Moreover, the exclusion and regulation of those who viewed the games emphasised the inhabitant's position in the city. This is most apparent when we consider the position of women and slaves: in the amphitheatre they were excluded, whilst in the theatres they were confined to the rear. In contrast, the magistrates of the city were located closest to the place of performance. It was here that the festivals were celebrated and, by that celebration, the spaces associated with the amphitheatre and theatres were made sacred. The use of sacred space, in ritual performance, varied from city to city. Ritual could celebrate a city's history or myth, or the myths associated with particular deities who had special meaning for the inhabitants of a particular city. In its festivals, a city emphasised its identity. However, overriding this unique identity of the individual city was its association with a common Roman present. This was emphasised with reference to the festivals associated with the Capitoline triad, Jupiter, Juno and Minerva, and the imperial cult. In Pompeii, the unique identity of the city was emphasised through the position of Venus. Often, however, it would have been impossible for the inhabitant to distinguish objectively which ritual associated them with Rome, and which expressed their uniqueness as a Pompeian. Naturally, the two were intertwined in this city in Campania that had become a Roman colony.

The city as an element distinct from the countryside is a consistent image in Western thought (Williams 1973). The inhabitants of Pompeii may well have considered themselves to be differentiated from those who lived in the countryside outside the city. The city walls, guarded by the *Lares*, defined the bounds of the city. A series of stones outside the gates marked the boundary of the city's *pomerium*. You could either be within or outside the city. The dead were buried outside the city. There was a clear symbolic division here, as well as two clearly defined spaces marked by the physical presence of the city wall. The meaning of this boundary around the city is not easy to understand. The inhabitants of the countryside regularly visited the city; equally, those living in the city may have visited the countryside and towns close by, such as Nuceria. Therefore, the boundary is permeable. The city has a close relationship to its rural hinterland in pre-industrial societies, particularly when the city does not cover a large area or have a large population. However, it would appear that cities were sacred places differentiated from the countryside. Their boundaries were sanctified; the city was a space which excluded the dead and contained not only a population but also a mythical and historical past. It was a node in the landscape that had a series of accumulated meanings, unlike the countryside, which had few places that had a meaningful past to those travelling through it. Cities had a history, whereas the countryside had none. Myth in the countryside was associated with the taming of nature. For example, the giants, so strongly associated with Vesuvius, were defeated by Hercules, who later brought the land under cultivation (Diod. 4.21; Dio 56.21–3). Features of the landscape, for example volcanoes, also gave the countryside meaning. In contrast, the city had meaning because of the actions of its inhabitants in the past and in the present.

However, those actions included the inhabitants of the city's rural hinterland, because collective action and decision making took place in the city. The rural inhabitants also associated themselves with the city and saw themselves as part of that community. The city played a major part in their lives as the place to which produce was taken, the place at which markets were held, the place at which the major festivals were celebrated. In fact, the city cannot be removed or isolated from its rural hinterland. The people of the countryside fundamentally associated themselves with their local city, and their identity was bound up with it. They were a regular feature of the city's *durée*, at markets, festivals and other events. Their history and identity involved the city at all levels. Equally, we cannot say that the inhabitants of the city were isolated from the countryside, because the rural inhabitants were a prominent feature in the city as regular visitors. The urban inhabitant may have known these people and where they were from. Indeed, in terms of local geography, the countryside was not an alien world, but as familiar as the geography of the city. In effect, we cannot divide the city from the countryside, or the countryside from the city. They are both part of the Roman conceptual landscape.

To a certain extent, it is the way in which this conceptual landscape was used that begins to define the city. There was a structure underlying an individual's actions and use of the city. This tends to be associated with a society's spatio-temporal dialectic (Giddens 1984: 17). An individual's actions were bound up with their notions of time, when it happened, and space, where it happened. For example, a religious festival took place in the city, space, at a certain date, time. Equally, markets were held on a weekly basis in Pompeii (Frayn 1993: 40; MacMullen 1970). This would have caused many people who may not have used the city otherwise to come to Pompeii on market day. For the elite, the daily cycle was dominated by the meeting of clients at the *salutatio*, followed by business in the forum, followed by bathing and finally dinner. Others may have worked from dawn to dusk with a break at midday (the sixth hour). This daily pattern would have been broken at festivals and other public holidays. However, the daily cycle of timed activities would have structured the day and the use of the city. For example, the baths were at their hottest at the sixth hour, but only the elite had the *otium* to utilise the baths at that hour, when the majority of the urban population were still working. In contrast, at a festival, the city would have been full of people from the countryside, the urban population and the elite enjoying their free time. People used the city in different ways at festivals, compared with their normal *durée* of everyday life. Moreover, people of unequal status used the city in different ways on a daily basis. In fact, the city structured itself to allow for this: the baths were at their hottest when the elite used them at the sixth hour, but at their coolest at the tenth or later, when the *mercennarius* managed to reach them after a day's work; we might doubt whether the *mercennarius* ever found time to bathe. Therefore, the timing of activities created a distance between the elite and others. There was also a spatial aspect to how people used the city. Each action in the elite's day was separate from the previous action: they left home for the forum, from the forum they went to the baths, and from the baths they went home to dine. In contrast, the urban inhabitant worked close to their place of residence with little cause to move far beyond it.

The elite ranged further across the city and utilised its resources to their optimum advantage. However, for the majority of the population activity was confined to the locality of their place of residence. The *durée* of their lives was limited and closer to home. Seldom would they have needed to stray far to find all their daily needs. Their local identity was bound up with that of their neighbours and concentrated upon the neighbourhood shrine to the *Lares*. The provision of a public fountain in the locality may have reinforced this division of the city into a series of *locales*. These *locales* should not be seen as socially homogeneous: the inhabitants might vary in status and wealth. Members of the elite did not segregate their place of residence from the place of residence of others of lower status. Other members of the *locale* may have been *magistri vici* or clients of others. It should be noted that the elite may not have drawn support in the form of clients from a single locality within the city. To gain the widest support, a person would have had clients from a wide range of geographical and social locations. Clients identified with the interests of their patrons; indeed, their lives and use of the city were bound up with the actions of their patron. For example, clients could have been expected to accompany their patron until the ninth hour. However, they would still have identified with their own *locale*, where their own importance as a client of X may have added to their status. The slaves in the city may not have ventured far from the household; indeed, a slave's social action was constrained by the demands of their owner. Slaves were prominent in the household and involved in work in the household, or tasks associated with it. Their knowledge and use of the city were controlled by the needs of their owner and their household. Those slaves employed to work in bakeries, for example, were tied to a similar time schedule to that of the *mercennarius*. Therefore, the slaves' use of the city was limited by the constraints placed upon them by their owner (see examples in Columella, book 11). The use of the city by women and children is problematic given the nature of our male-orientated sources. Women who worked would have followed a structure similar to that of the male *mercennarius*. If employed in the *popinae*, they would have worked during and just before opening and just after closing. For elite females, activity may well have been centred upon the household, once the adult males had left after the *salutatio*. Women bathed separately from men in Pompeii, in a set of baths that were on a smaller scale than those designed for men. Therefore, in the Roman city, there was a whole series of individuals using the city in different ways, at a variety of times during the day, and in different ways on certain days. This cumulative pattern of use defined the city itself. In other words, the Roman city can be defined by the way the inhabitants and visitors used it.

The spatial organisation of this pattern reflects the use of the city in its temporal framework. The forum was the centre of public activity. The major through-routes leading from the city gates to the forum were the major arteries of activity. Shops tended to be located on the through-routes. This pattern describes the strong link between the city and the countryside. Workshops were distributed throughout the city, but there was a stronger concentration of workshops in *Regio 7*, to the east of the forum. Inns tended to be located close to the city gates, or in the heart of the city to the east of the forum. The purpose-built brothels were also located in this area. In fact, the area to the east of the forum was the integrating core of the city. The network of narrow irregular streets linked the major through-routes together. The area was isolated from the residences of the elite, and in many ways, it may have been seen as morally corrupting. However, for many using the city, this area was the location of the pleasures of city life; moreover, there was a concentration of small-scale craft production in it. Much was located here that the elite found sordid, so that for them, it was important to have a house that was located upon a through-route, or one of the wider streets, such as Via di Mercurio. Their view of the city may have avoided the central area to the east of the forum. It was for the aediles to police this area of moral corruption. The elite distanced themselves from this area of the city; although the rear of some *atrium* houses backed on to this area, the *atrium* house was designed to be viewed from the *fauces*. Thus, it can be concluded that the elite structured their lives around a series of formal activities (the *salutatio*, the forum, the baths and dining). The daily routine of the rest of the population was confined to their *locale*, with forays into other parts of the city for resources and recreation unavailable in their neighbourhood. Similarly, the inhabitant of the countryside came to the city to acquire resources and recreation that they could not provide for themselves.

Models such as the consumer or service city fail to account for this complexity by reducing all social activity to its economic function. The Roman city had an important social aspect. The city in Roman society was a surplus product, which formed the means of Roman social reproduction; in effect, it was part of the means of production in Roman Italy. It was the place in which politics, economics, history, myth and *urbanitas* were concentrated. To discuss the Roman Empire without reference to the city is to miss the point. The Roman Empire was made up of cities; hence to define the city is to define Roman society. However, the city should never be viewed as isolated from the countryside, which was part of the city. In the end, we must say that the Roman city consisted of the social actions of its inhabitants and visitors in space and time. These were inscribed upon the fabric of the city, and they accumulated to produce urban formations such as Pompeii upon the eve of its destruction in AD 79.

NOTES

INTRODUCTION

1 Note that he regards his sample of *Regio* 1 as representative of all of Pompeii. Although the control, a sample of *Regio* 6, validates this argument, it should be noted that his predictive sample of *Regio* 1 and his control *Regio* 6 need not be representative of the whole city of Pompeii. If *Regio* 7 or 8 had been used as the control sample some rather different conclusions about the sampling strategy would have been made apparent.

2 Wallace-Hadrill 1990: 157 points out that 1.6.13 and 1.9.8/9/10 were deserted, but until there is an adequate study of the finds, we shall be unable to assess the extent of abandonment adequately. For comparison, in late medieval Coventry 25 per cent of all houses were empty.

3 In particular, problems arise from literary descriptions of Campanian agriculture: Plin., *N.H.* 3.60; Strabo 5.4.3, 5.4.8; Varro, *R.R.* 1.2.4, 1.20.4. Assertions of these sources are discredited via reference to early modern census returns.

4 See in particular Jongman 1988: 137–54, where he uses a combination of location theory and census data from an early modern context to offer a conclusive application of the 'consumer city' model.

1 ANCIENT AND MODERN TOWN PLANNING

1 Fully recorded in *Transactions of Town Planning Conference, London, 10–15 October 1910* (London, RIBA, 1911).

2 ibid.

2 PUBLIC BUILDING AND URBAN IDENTITY

1 For the dating of buildings, I use established dates. It should be noted that the dating of Pompeian buildings is not absolute and that controversy abounds.

2 With a *terminus ante quem* of 78 BC. See *CIL* 4.1842 for the basilica. For discussion see Laidlaw 1985:39 and Strocka 1991: 101. For the *macellum* see De Ruyt 1983: 137–40.

3 Mouritsen 1988: 86–7 emends the text to read *ambitio*. This is not really convincing: see Wiseman 1977 for discussion of the meaning of *ambulatio* in this context.

4 Their circular form would have diffused the forces, unlike a rectangular temple, which would have buckled.

3 LOCAL IDENTITY:
NEIGHBOURS AND NEIGHBOURHOODS

1 There are good parallels for this, for example in Rome. *CIL* 6.975 has *vici* named after the Porta Naevia and Porta Rudusculana.

2 But note that *ILLRP* 200 refers to some *Lares Augusti* dated to 59 BC at Rome. However, in this example there is no reference to *magistri*. Therefore, it seems likely that the *magistri Augusti* were an imperial innovation within the structure of an existing cult.

3 Suetonius states categorically that Augustus divided the city with no reference to an earlier division of Rome into *vici*. Compare with Dion. Hal. 4.14, connecting the division to Servius Tullius.

4 It should be noted that the recording of history in the epigraphic record is subject to a number of variables. The prominence of the *Pagus Augustus Felix Suburbanus* may be accounted for by the wealth of its magistrates relative to the wealth of magistrates of other *vici* and *pagi*.

5 Many of the paintings have now faded, and we rely upon earlier accounts for their description: Mau 1899: 233–6; Fiorelli 1875: 81, 82, 108, 175, 214, 249, 273, 303, 324, 343; *NS* 1911: 417–24.

6 The *Regionaries* significantly record the same number of *vici* and *aedicula* in each region in Rome.

7 In Petr., *Sat.* 70 slaves carried water in *amphorae* in Trimalchio's house. It is unclear whether they drew the water from a public or private fountain.

8 e.g. 8.3.6 on poor-quality water in Athens suitable only for the baths, whilst well water was used for drinking. It is worth noting that Vitruvius was involved in the distribution of water in Rome, Front., *Aqu.* 25. Front., *Aqu.* 2.92 suggests that, in Rome, good-quality water should be reserved for drinking, whereas poor-quality water should be used for bathing, fulling and other purposes.

9 Front., *Aqu.* 1.12 cannot understand why Augustus brought the Alsietinian aqueduct to Rome, because the water was not suitable for human consumption. Front., *Aqu.* 2.93 illustrates the efforts under Trajan to obtain clear water.

10 These figures do not account for the velocity of flow, but represent a clear perception of an ancient expert upon water.

11 Rainwater is frequently utilised as well: see Vitr. 8.2. For use of public and private supplies see Snow 1965.

12 The figure would have been higher had not many people fled.

4 PRODUCTION AND CONSUMPTION

1 For an excellent introduction to the study of *amphorae* see Peacock and Williams 1986. Note also the possibilities for the reuse of *amphorae* (Callendar 1965: 30–6).

2 Remnants of these workshops confirm Moeller's original definition of the location of production.

3 Today market gardening appears as an urban phenomenon in most Campanian towns.

5 DEVIANT BEHAVIOUR

1 Corbin 1990: 4–10 examines the regulation and marginalisation of prostitution in nineteenth-century France; Cohen 1980 documents the conditions in which prostitution may be tolerated in one street but not in a neighbouring area.

2 Pliny, in his address to Trajan, states that it was an emperor's use of his *otium* that

betrayed his true character, and he states that unlike his predecessors, Trajan did not gamble. On the other hand, Suetonius tells us that Augustus, Caligula, Claudius, Nero, Vitellius and Domitian all gambled (Plin., *Paneg.* 82.8–9; Suet., *Aug.* 70–1, *Cal.* 41, *Claud.* 33; Sen., *Apocol.* 15; Suet., *Nero* 30; *Vit.* 4, *Dom.* 21).

7 THE PRODUCTION OF SPACE

1 For a reconstruction of the early street plan of the original sixth century BC see Ward-Perkins (1974), figs 40–1. I would personally favour a less regular arrangement. However, recently Nappo (1988) has demonstrated that the *insulae* of *Regiones* 1 and 2 were of considerable antiquity also in their layout.
2 It is notable that Vicolo degli Scheletri and Vicolo del Balcone Pensile were curtailed by the development of monumental structures in the forum.
3 I use the terms in the broadest sense. For a full explanation of the concept see Champion (1989) in the context of inter-site studies.

8 THE TEMPORAL LOGIC OF SPACE

1 For a formal experiment in gender-based encounter patterns see Hillier and Hanson 1984: 223–41.
2 Suet., *Galba* 4 states that Galba adhered to the obsolete custom of wishing his slaves good night and good morning.
3 Unfortunately, this space–time pattern cannot be reconstructed, because there are insufficent data.

BIBLIOGRAPHY

Adam, J.P. (1980) *Dégradation et restauration de l'architecture pompéienne*, Paris.

Allison, P.M. (1992a) 'The relationship between wall-decoration and room-type in Pompeian houses: a case study of the Casa della Caccia Antica', *Journal of Roman Archaeology* 5: 235–49.

—— (1992b) 'Artefact assemblages: not "the Pompeii Premise"', in E. Herring, R. Whitehouse and J. Wilkins (eds) *Papers of the Fourth Conference of Italian Archaeology 3: New Developments in Italian Archaeology* 49–56, London.

Ambrose, J. and Vergun, D. (1980) *Simplified Building Design for Wind and Earthquake Forces*, New York.

Andreau, J. (1973) 'Histoire des séismes et histoire économique: le tremblement de terre de Pompéi (62 ap.J-C.)', *Annales ESC* 28: 369–95.

—— (1974) *Les Affaires de Monsieur Jucundus*, Rome.

—— (1980) 'Pompéi: mais où sont les vétérans de Sylla?', *Revue Etudes Anciennes* 82: 183–99.

—— (1984) 'Il terremoto del 62', in F. Zevi (ed.) *Pompei 79. Raccolta per il decimo centenario dell'eruzione Vesuviana*, Napoli.

Arthur, P. (1986) 'Problems of the urbanisation of Pompeii', *Antiquaries Journal* 66: 29–44.

Ashworth, W. (1965) *The Genesis of Modern Town Planning*, London.

Atkinson, D. (1914) 'A hoard of Samian ware from Pompeii', *Journal of Roman Studies* 4: 27–64.

Ayeni, B. (1979) *Concepts and Techniques in Urban Analysis*, London.

Balsdon, J.P.V.D. (1969) *Life and Leisure in Ancient Rome*, London.

Barthes, R. (1986) 'Semiology and the urban', in M. Gottdiener and A. Ph. Lagopoulos (eds) *The City and the Sign. An Introduction to Urban Semiotics*, New York.

Beacham, J.R.C. (1991) *The Roman Theatre and its Audience*, London.

Becker, H.S. (1987) 'Outsiders', in E. Rubinstein and M.S. Wennberg (eds) *Deviance: The Interactionist Perspective*, New York.

Boardman, P. (1978) *The Worlds of Patrick Geddes*, London.

Bonghi Jovino, M. (1984) *Ricerche à Pompei l'insula 5 della Regio VI dalle origini al 79 d.C.*, Roma.

Buckland, W.W. (1921) *A Text-book of Roman Law from Augustus to Justinian*, Cambridge.

Bulmer, M. (1986) *Neighbours. The Work of Philip Abrams*, Cambridge.

Callendar, M.H. (1965) *Roman Amphorae*, Oxford.

Carandini, A. (1977) *L'instrumentum domesticum di Ercolano e Pompei nella prima età imperiale*, Roma.

—— (1988) *Schiavi in Italia. Gli strumenti pensanti dei Romani fra tarda Repubblica e medio Impero*, Roma.

Carlstein, T. (1982) *Time Resources, Society and Ecology. On the Capacity for Human Interaction in Space and Time. Volume 1: Preindustrial*, London.

Carocci, F., de Albentis, E., Gargiuto, M. and Pesando, F. (1990) *Le Insulae 3 e 4 della Regio VI di Pompei*, Roma.

Castells, M. (1977) *The Urban Question: A Marxist Approach*, London.

Castiglione, V., Del Franco, M. and Vitale, R. (1989) 'L'insula 8 della Regio 1: un campione d'indagine socio-economica', *Rivista di Studi Pompeiane* 3: 185–221.

Castiglione Morelli, N. (1983) 'Le lucerne della casa di Giulio Polibio à Pompei', *Bollettino dell'Associazione Internazionale Amici di Pompei* 1: 213–58.

Castrén, P. (1975) *Ordo Populusque Pompeianus. Polity and Society in Roman Pompeii*, Roma.

Cerulli Irelli, G. (1977) 'Officina di lucerne fittili à Pompei', in *L'instrumentum domesticum di Ercolani e Pompei nella prima età imperiale*, Roma.

Champion, T.C. (1989) *Centre and Periphery. Comparative Studies in Archaeology*, London.

Cherry, G.E. (1988) *Cities and Plans. The Shaping of Britain in the Nineteenth and Twentieth Centuries*, London.

Chiaramonte Treré, C. (1986) *Nuovi contributi sulle fortificazioni Pompeiane*, Milano.

Clarke, J.R. (1991) *The Houses of Roman Italy 100 BC–AD 250: Ritual, Space and Decoration*, Berkeley.

Coarelli, F. (1980) *Roma. Guide archeoligiche Laterza*, Bari.

Cohen, B. (1980) *Deviant Street Networks: Prostitution in New York City*, Toronto.

Cohen, D. (1991) 'The Augustan law on adultery: the social and cultural context', in D.I. Kertzer and R.P. Saller (eds) *The Family in Italy from Antiquity to the Present*, New Haven.

Cohen, S. (1985) *Visions of Social Control*, Cambridge.

Coleman, K.M. (1990) 'Fatal charades: Roman executions staged as mythological enactments', *Journal of Roman Studies* 80: 44–73.

Connolly, P. (1979) *Pompeii*, London.

Conticello, B. (1990) *Rediscovering Pompeii*, exhibition catalogue, Roma.

Corbin, A. (1990) *Women for Hire. Prostitution and Sexuality in France after 1850*, London.

Coulton, J.J. (1987) 'Roman aqueducts in Asia Minor', in S. Macready and F.H. Thompson (eds) *Roman Architecture in the Greek World*, London.

Crawford, M.H. (1969) *Roman Republican Coin Hoards*, London.

—— (1970) 'Money and exchange in the Roman world', *Journal of Roman Studies* 60: 40–8.

Crook, J.A. (1967) *Law and Life of Rome*, London.

Curtis, R.I. (1979) 'The Garum shop of Pompeii (1.12.8)', *Cronache Pompeiane* 5: 5–23.

—— (1983) 'In defense of Garum', *Classical Journal* 78: 232–48.

—— (1984a) 'A personalised floor mosaic from Pompeii', *American Journal of Archaeology* 88: 557–66.

—— (1984b) 'The salted fish industry of Pompeii', *Archaeology* 37, 58 and 74.

—— (1985) 'Product identification and advertising on Roman commercial amphorae', *Ancient Society* 16: 209–28.

—— (1991) *Garum and Salsamenta. Production and Commerce in Maleria Medica*, Leiden.

Dalby, A.F. (1972) *Small Buildings in Earthquake Areas*, Watford.

D'Ambrosio, A. and Borriello, M. (1990) *Le terrecotte figurate di Pompei*, Roma.

D'Ambrosio, A. and De Caro, S. (1983) 'La necropoli di Porta Nocera', in L. Vlad Borelli, F. Parise Badoni, O. Ferrari, A. D'Ambrosio and S. De Caro, *Un impegno per Pompei* 23–42, Milano.

D'Arms, J.H. (1970) *Romans on the Bay of Naples. A Social and Cultural Study of the Villas and their Owners from 150 BC to AD 400*, Cambridge, Mass.

—— (1981) *Commerce and Social Standing in Ancient Rome*, Cambridge.

D'Arms, J.H. and Kopff, E.C. (1980) *The Seabourne Commerce of Ancient Rome. Studies in Archaeology and History*, published as *Memoirs of the American Academy at Rome 36*.

De Caro, S. (1974) 'Le lucerne dell'officina LVC', *Rendiconti dell'Academia di Archeologia Lettere e Belli Arti di Napoli* 49: 107–34.

—— (1985) 'Nuove indagini sulle fortificazioni di Pompei', *Annali dell'Instituto Universitario Orientale di Napoli* 7: 75–114.

—— (1986) *Saggi nell'area del tempio di Apollo à Pompei*, Napoli.

De Franciscis, A. (1976) 'Sepolcro di M. Obellius Firmus', *Cronache Pompeiana* 2: 246–8.

Degrassi, A. (1935) 'Sui fasti di *Magisti Vici* rinvenuti in Via Marmorata', *Bullettino della Commissione Archeologia Communale di Roma* 43: 173–8.

—— (1947) *Inscriptiones Italiae* 13.1, Roma.

Della Corte, M. (1913) 'Il *pomerium* di Pompei', *RendLincei* 22: 261–2.

—— (1928) 'Pompei-Borgo Marinaio', *Notizie degli Scavi* 369–72.

—— (1965) *Case ed abitanti di Pompei*, 3rd edition, Napoli.

De Ruyt, C. (1983) *Macellum. Marché alimentaire des romains*, Louvain.

Descœudres, J.P. and Sear, F. (1987) 'The Australian expedition to Pompeii', *Rivista di Studi Pompeieane* 1: 11–36.

Deutsche, R. (1991) 'Boys Town', *Environment and Planning D: Society and Space* 9: 5–30.

Dixon, S. (1992) *The Roman Family*, Baltimore.

Döhl, H. and Zanker, P. (1984) 'La scultura', in F. Zevi (ed.) *Pompei 79. Racolta per il decimo centenario dell'eruzione Vesuviana*, Napoli.

Dowdall, H.C. and Adshead, S.D. (1910) 'The Town Planning Act 1909', *Town Planning Review* 1: 39–50.

Duncan-Jones, R.P. (1982) *The Economy of the Roman Empire: Quantitative Studies*, Cambridge.

Dwyer, E. (1991) 'The Pompeian atrium house in theory and in practice', in E.K. Gazda (ed.) *Roman Art in the Private Sphere*, Ann Arbor.

Dyson, S.L. (1993) 'From new to new age archaeology: archaeological theory and classical archaeology – a 1990s perspective', *American Journal of Archaeology* 97: 195–206.

Ehrhardt, W. (1988) *Casa dell'Orso (VII 2, 44–46)*, München.

Engels, D. (1990) *Roman Corinth. An Alternative Model for the Classical City*, Chicago.

Eschebach, H. (1973) 'Untersuchungen in den Stabianer Thermen zu Pompeji', *Mitteilungen des Deutschen Archaeologischen Instituts Römische* 80: 235–42.

—— (1979) 'Probleme der Wasserversorgung Pompejis', *Cronache Pompeiane* 5: 24–60.

—— (1982) 'Die Casa di Ganimede in Pompeji VII 13,4', *Mitteilungen des Deustchen Archaeologischen Instituts Römische* 89: 229–436.

Eschebach, H. and Schäfer, T. (1983) 'Die Öeffentlichen Laufbrunnen Pompejis Katalog und Beschreibung', *Bulletino di Associazione Internazionale Amici di Pompei* 1: 11–40.

Etienne, R. (1992) *Pompeii: The Day a City Died*, London.

Fienga, F. (1932/3) 'Esplorazione del pago marittino Pompeiana', in *Atti dell'III Congresso Nazionale di Studi Romani* 11: 172–6.

Finley, M. (1973) *The Ancient Economy*, London.

Fiorelli, G. (1875) *Descrizione di Pompei*, Napoli.

Flambard, J.M. (1977) 'Clodius, les collèges, la plèbe et les esclaves', *Mélanges d'Archeologie et d'Histoire de l'Ecole Française de Rome* 89: 115–56.

—— (1981) '*Collegia compitalicia*: phénomène associatif, cadres territoriaux et cadres civiques dans le monde Romain à l'époque républicaine', *Ktema* 6: 143–66.

Foucault, M. (1977) *Discipline and Punish. The Birth of the Prison*, London.

—— (1984a) 'Space, knowledge and power', in P. Rabinow (ed.) *The Foucault Reader*, London.

—— (1984b) *The Care of the Self. History of Sexuality* vol. 3, London.

Franklin, J.L. (1987) 'Pantomimists at Pompeii: Actius Anicetus and his troupe', *American Journal of Philology* 108: 95–107.

—— (1990) *Pompeii: The 'Casa del Marinaio' and its History*, Roma.

Frayn, J.M. (1993) *Markets and Fairs in Roman Italy*, Oxford.

Frederiksen, M. (1980/1) 'Puteoli e il commercio del grano in epoca romana', *Puteoli* 4–5: 5–27.

—— (1984) *Campania*, Oxford.

Fröhlich T. (1991) *Lararien- und Fassadenbilder in den Vesuvstädten: Untersuchungen zur 'Volkstümlichen' Pompejanischen Malerei*, Mainz am Rhein.

Gardner, J.F. (1986) *Women in Roman Law and Society*, London.

Garnsey, P. (1970) *Social Status and Legal Privilege in the Roman Empire*, Oxford.

—— (1988) *Famine and the Food Supply in the Graeco-Roman World*, Cambridge.

Gibbs, S.L. (1976) *Greek and Roman Sundials*, Berkeley.

Giddens, A. (1981) *A Contemporary Critique of Historical Materialism*, London.

—— (1984) *The Constitution of Society*, Oxford.

Gigante, M. (1979) *Civiltà delle forme letterarie nell'antica Pompei*, Napoli.

Goodie, E. (1984) *Deviant Behaviour*, Englewood Cliffs.

Gralfs, B. (1988) *Metallverarbeitende Produktionsstätten in Pompeji*, BAR International Series 433, Oxford.

Grassner, V. (1986) 'Die Kaufläden in Pompeii', Dissertationen der Universität Wien.

Greene, K. (1986) *The Archaeology of the Roman Economy*, London.

—— (1992) *Roman Pottery*, London.

Guidoboni, E. (1989) *I terremoti prima del mille in Italia e nell'area mediterranea*, Bologna.

Hardy, D. (1991) *From Garden Cities to New Towns. Campaigning for Town and Country Planning 1899–1946*, London.

Harmand, L. (1957) *Le Patronat sur les collectivités publiques*, Louvain.

Harris, W.V. (1980) 'Roman terracotta lamps: the organisation of an industry', *Journal of Roman Studies* 70: 126–45.

Harrison, M. (1986) 'The ordering of the urban environment: time, work and the occurrence of crowds 1790–1835', *Past and Present* 110: 134–68.

Harvey, D. (1988) *Social Justice and the City*, Oxford.

—— (1990) *The Condition of Postmodernity*, Oxford.

Haverfield, F. (1910) 'Town planning in the Roman world', in *Transactions of the Town Planning Conference, London, 10–15 October 1910*, London, RIBA.

—— (1913) *Ancient Town Planning*, Oxford.

Herbert, D.T. and Thomas, C.J. (1982) *Urban Geography: A First Approach*, London.

Hermansen, G. (1978) 'The population of imperial Rome: the *regionaries*', *Historia* 27: 129–68.

—— (1981) *Ostia: Aspects of City Life*, Edmonton.

Hillier, B. and Hanson, J. (1984) *The Social Logic of Space*, Cambridge.

Hopkins, K. (1978) 'Economic growth and towns in classical antiquity', in P. Abrams and E.A. Wrigley (eds) *Towns in Societies*, Cambridge.

—— (1983) *Death and Renewal. Sociological Studies in Roman History*, vol. 2, Cambridge.

Ioppolo, G. (1992) *Le Terme del Sarno a Pompei*, Roma.

Jansen, G.C.M. (1991) 'Water systems and sanitation in the houses of Herculaneum', *Mededelingen van het Nederlands Institut te Rome* 50: 145–66.

Jashemski, W. (1964) 'A Pompeian copa', *Classical Journal* 59: 337–49.

—— (1979) *The Gardens of Pompeii*, New York.

Jongman, W. (1988) *The Economy and Society of Pompeii*, Amsterdam.

Kampen, N. (1981) *Image and Status: Roman Working Women in Ostia*, Berlin.

Kleberg, T. (1957) *Hôtels, restaurants et cabarets dans l'antique romaine: études historiques et philologiques*, Uppsala.

Klejn, L.S. (1993) 'To separate a centaur: on the relationship of archaeology and history in Soviet tradition', *Antiquity* 67: 339–48.

Laidlaw, A. (1985) *The First Style in Pompeii: Painting and Architecture*, Roma.

Landes, D.S. (1987) 'Ordering the urban environment: time, work and the occurrence of crowds 1790–1835', *Past and Present* 116: 192–8.

La Torre, G.F. (1988) 'Gli impianti commerciali ed artigianali nel tessuto urbano di Pompei' in Franchi dell'Orto (ed.) *Pompei l'informatica al servizio di una città antica*, Roma.

Laurence, R. (1991) 'The urban *vicus*: the spatial organisation of power in the Roman city', in E. Herring, R. Whitehouse and J. Wilkins (eds) *The Archaeology of Power*, vol.1, London.

Lefebvre, H. (1991) *The Production of Space*, Oxford.

Le Goff, P. (1960) 'Au moyen âge: temps de l'église et temps au marchand', *Annales ESC* 15: 417–33.

Leppmann, W. (1968) *Pompeii in Fact and Fiction*, London.

Ling, R. (1983) 'The Insula of the Menander at Pompeii: an interim report', *Antiquaries' Journal* 63: 34–57.

—— (1990) 'A stranger in town: finding the way in an ancient city', *Greece and Rome* 14: 157–70.

—— (1991) 'The architecture of Pompeii', *Journal of Roman Archaeology* 4: 248–55.

MacDonald, W.L. (1986) *The Architecture of the Roman Empire II: An Urban Appraisal*, New Haven.

MacMullen, R. (1970) 'Market-days in the Roman Empire', *Phoenix* 24: 333–41.

Maiuri, A. (1942) *L'ultima fase edilizia di Pompei*, Roma.

—— (1973) *Alla ricerca di Pompei preromana*, Napoli.

Manacorda, D. (1977) 'Anfore spagnole à Pompei', *L'instrumentum domesticum di Ercolano e Pompei*, Roma.

Mancini, G. (1935) 'Fasti consolari e censorii ed elenco di *Vicomagistri* rinvenuti in Via Marmorea', *Bullettino della Commissione Archeologia Communale di Roma* 43: 35–79

Massey, D. (1991) 'Flexible sexism', *Environment and Planning D: Society and Space* 9: 31–57.

Matthews, J. (1989) *The Roman Empire of Ammianus*, London.

Mau, A. (1899) *Pompeii: Its Life and Art*, Washington.

Mayeske, B.J.B. (1972) 'Bakeries, bakers and bread at Pompeii: a study in social and economic history', Ph.D. thesis, Maryland.

Meiggs, R. (1973) *Roman Ostia*, Oxford.

Meller, H. (1990) *Patrick Geddes: Social Evolutionist and City Planner*, London.

Michel, D. (1990) *Casa dei Cei (I 6, 15)*, München.

Miller, M. (1992) *Raymond Unwin: Garden Cities and Town Planning*, Leicester.

Moeller, W.O. (1975) 'The date and dedication of the building of Eumachia', *Cronache Pompeiana* 1: 232–6.

—— (1976) *The Wool Trade of Ancient Pompeii*, Leiden.

Morris, A.S. (1987) 'Mendoza. Land use in the Adobe City', in C.S. Yadav (ed.) *The Morphology of Towns*, New Delhi.

Mouritsen, H. (1988) *Elections, Magistrates and Municipal Elite. Studies in Pompeian Epigraphy*, Roma.

—— (1990) 'A note on Pompeian epigraphy and social structure', *Classica et Mediaevalia* 61: 131–49.

—— (forthcoming) 'Order and disorder in late Pompeian politics', in *Les Elites municipales de l'Italie péninsulaire des Grecques à Nérone*, Clermont Ferrand.

Mumford, L. (1961) *The City in History*, Harmondsworth.

Mustilli, D. (1950) 'Botteghe di scultori, marmorarii, bronzieri e caelatores in Pompei', in A. Maiuri (ed.) *Pompeiana*, Napoli.

Mygind, H. (1917) 'Die Wasserversorgung Pompejis', *Janus* 21: 294–351.

—— (1921) 'Hygienische Verhältnisse im alten Pompeji', *Janus* 25: 251–383.

Nappo, S.C. (1988) 'Regio I Insula 20', *Rivista di Studi Pompeiane* 2: 186–92.

Nielsen, I. (1990) *Thermae et Balnea. The Architecture and Cultural History of Roman Public Baths*, Aarhus.

Nippel, W. (1984) 'Policing Rome', *Journal of Roman Studies* 74: 20–30.

Nishida, Y. (1991) 'Measuring structures in Pompeii', *Opuscula Pompeiana* 1: 91–102.

Nishida, Y. and Hori, Y. (1992) 'The investigations of *Regio* VII *Insula* 12', *Opuscula Pompeiana* 2: 48–72.

Ostrow, A.K. (1990) *The Sarno Bath Complex*, Roma.

Owens, E.J. (1989) 'Roman town planning', in I.M. Barton (ed.) *Roman Public Buildings*, Exeter.

—— (1991) *The City in the Greek and Roman World*, London.

Packer, J.E. (1971) *The Insulae of Imperial Ostia*, published as Memoirs of the American Academy at Rome 31.

—— (1978) 'Inns at Pompeii: a short survey', *Cronache Pompeiane* 4: 5–53.

Panella, C. (1974/5) 'Per uno studio delle anfore di Pompei. Le forme 8 e 10 della tipologia di R. Schoene', *Studi Miscellanei* 22: 149–62.

—— (1981) 'La distribuzione e i mercati', in A. Giardina and A. Schiavone (eds) *Società Romana e Produzione Schiavistica*, vol. 2, 55–80.

Panella, C. and Fano, M. (1974/5) 'Le anfore con anse bifide conservate a Pompei, contributo ad uno loro classificazione', in G. Vallet (ed.) *Méthodes classiques et méthodes formelles dans l'étude des amphores*, Roma.

Peacock, D.P.S. (1977) 'Pompeian Red Ware', in D.P.S. Peacock (ed.) *Pottery and Early Commerce: Characterisation and Trade in Roman and Later Ceramics*, London.

—— (1980) 'The Roman millstone trade: a petrological sketch', *World Archaeology* 12: 43–53.

—— (1982) *Pottery in the Roman World: An Ethnoarchaeological Approach*, London.

—— (1986) 'The production of millstones near Orvieto, Umbria, Italy', *Antiquaries Journal* 66: 45–51.

—— (1989) 'The mills of Pompeii', *Antiquity* 63: 205–14.

Peacock, D.P.S. and Williams, D.F. (1986) *Amphorae and the Roman Economy*, London.

Pelling, M. (1978) *Cholera, Fever and English Medicine 1825–1865*, Oxford.

Peters, W.J.J. (1993) *La casa di Marcus Lucretius Fronto à Pompei e le sue pitture*, Amsterdam.

Porteous, J.D. (1977) *Environment and Behavior: Planning and Everyday Urban Life*, Reading, Mass.

Pucci, G. (1977) 'Le terre sigillate Italiche, Galliche e Orientali', in *L'instrumentum domesticum di Ercolano e Pompei nella prima età imperiale*, Roma.

—— (1981) 'La ceramica Italica (terra sigillata)', in A. Giardina and A. Schiavone (eds) *Società Romana e Produzione Schiavistica*, vol. 2, Bari.

Raban, J. (1974) *Soft City*, London.

Raper, R.A. (1977) 'The analysis of the urban structure of Pompeii: a sociological study of land use', in D. Clarke (ed.) *Spatial Archaeology*, London.

Rawson, E. (1985) 'Theatrical life in Republican Rome and Italy', *Papers of the British School at Rome* 81: 97–113.

—— (1987) '*Discrimina Ordinum*: the *Lex Julia Theatralis*', *Papers of the British School at Rome* 55: 83–114.

Richardson, L. (1974) 'The archaic Doric temple of Pompeii', *La Parola del Passato* 29: 281–90.

—— (1978) 'Concordia and Concordia Augusta: Rome and Pompeii', *La Parola del Passato* 33: 260–72.

—— (1988) *Pompeii. An Architectural History*, Baltimore.

Rickman, G. (1980) *The Corn Supply of Rome*, Oxford.

Robinson, O. (1991) *Ancient Rome. City Planning and Administration*, London.

Rodriguez-Almeida, E. (1980) *Forma Urbis Marmorea: aggiornamento generale*, Roma.

Rossi, A. (1982) *Architecture and the City*, Cambridge, Mass.

Rostovtzeff, M. (1957) *Social and Economic History of the Roman Empire*, Oxford.

Rousselle, A. (1992) 'Body politics in ancient Rome', in P. Schmitt Pantel (ed.) *A History of Women in the West I: From Ancient Goddesses to Christian Saints*, London.

Rubington, E. and Wennberg, M.S. (1987) *Deviance: The Interactionist Perspective*, New York.

Ruddell, S.M. (1964) 'The inn, restaurant and tavern business in ancient Pompeii', M.A. thesis, University of Maryland.

Rykwert, J. (1976) *The Idea of a Town. The Anthropology of Urban Form in Rome, Italy and the Ancient World*, London.

Sakai, S. (1991) 'Some considerations of the urbanism in the so-called "Neustadt in Pompeii"', *Opuscula Pompeiana* 1: 35–57.

Salas, E. (1966) 'L'Evolution de la notion au temps et les horlogers à l'époque coloniale au Chili', *Annales ESC* 21: 141–58.

Saller, R.P. (1987) 'Men's age at marriage and its consequences in the Roman family', *Classical Philology* 82: 21–34.

—— (1991) Review of Engels 1990, *Classical Philology* 86: 351–7.

Saller, R.P. and Shaw, B.D. (1984) 'Roman tombstones and Roman family relations in the principate', *Journal of Roman Studies* 74: 124–57.

Saunders, P. (1986) *Social Theory and the Urban Question*, London.

Scheid, J. (1992) 'The religious roles of women', in P. Schmitt Pantel (ed.) *A History of Women I: From Ancient Goddesses to Christian Saints*, London, 377–408.

Searle, G.R. (1971) *The Quest for National Efficiency*, Oxford.

—— (1976) *Eugenics and Politics in Britain 1900–1914*, Leiden.

Seiler, F. (1992) *Casa degli Amorini Dorati (VI 16, 7.38)*, München.

Shaw, B.D. (1987) 'The age of Roman girls at marriage: some reconsiderations', *Journal of Roman Studies* 77: 30–46.

— (1991) 'The cultural meaning of death: age and gender in the Roman family', in D.I. Kertzer and R.P. Saller (eds) *The Family in Italy from Antiquity to the Present*, New Haven.

Sjoberg, G. (1960) *The Preindustrial City*, Glencoe.

Slane, K.W. (1989) 'Corinthian ceramic imports: the changing pattern of provincial trade in the first and second centuries A.D.', in S. Walker and A. Cameron (eds) *The Greek Renaissance in the Roman Empire*, BICS Supplement 55, London, 219–25.

Smith, M.P. (1992) 'Postmodernism, urban ethnography, and the new social space of ethnic identity', *Theory and Society* 24(4): 493–531.

Snow, J. (1965) *Snow on Cholera. Being a Reprint of Two Papers by John Snow*, New York.

Sogliano, A. (1901) 'Il Borgo Marinaio presso il Sarno', *Notizie degli Scavi* 423–40.

Soja, E.W. (1989) *Postmodern Geographies. The Reassertion of Space in Critical Social Theory*, London.

Solmsen, F. (1979) *Isis among the Greeks and Romans*, London.

Spinazzola, V. (1953) *Pompei alla luce degli scavi nuovi di Via dell'Abbondanza (anni 1910–1923)*, Roma.

Strocka, V.M. (1984) *Casa del principe di Napoli (VI 15.7–8)*, München.

— (1991) *Casa del labirinto (VI 11,8–10)*, München.

Tchernia, A. (1986) *Le Vin de l'Italie romaine*, Roma.

Thompson, E.P. (1967) 'Time, work-discipline and industrial capitalism', *Past and Present* 38: 56–97.

Todd, F.A. (1939) 'Three Pompeian wall-inscriptions and Petronius', *Classical Review* 53: 5–9.

Treggiari, S.M. (1980) 'Urban labour in Rome: *mercennarii* and *tabernarii*', in P. Garnsey (ed.) *Non-Slave Labour in the Greco-Roman World*, Cambridge.

Tsujimura, S. (1991) 'Ruts in Pompeii. The traffic system in the Roman city', *Opuscula Pompeiana* 2: 58–86.

Unwin, R. (1909) *Town Planning in Practice*, New York.

Vanderbroeck, P.J. (1987) *Popular Leadership and Collective Behaviour in the Late Roman Republic*, Amsterdam.

Verney, P. (1979) *The Earthquake Handbook*, London.

Veyne, P. (1990) *Bread and Circuses*, Harmondsworth.

Vlad Borelli, L., Parise Badoni, F., Ferrari, O., D'Ambrosio, A. and De Caro, S. (1983) *Un impegno per Pompei*, Milano.

Wallace-Hadrill, A. (1988) 'The social structure of the Roman house', *Papers of the British School at Rome* 56: 43–97.

— (1990) 'The social spread of Roman luxury: sampling Pompeii', *Papers of the British School at Rome* 58: 145–92.

— (1991) 'Houses and households: sampling Pompeii and Herculaneum', in B. Rawson, *Marriage, Divorce and Children in Ancient Rome*, Oxford.

— (1994) 'The urban texture of Pompeii', in T. Cornell and K. Lomas (eds) *Urban Society in Roman Italy*, London.

Walvin, J. (1978) *Leisure and Society, 1830–1950*, London.

Ward-Perkins, J.B. (1974) *Cities of Ancient Greece and Italy: Planning in Classical Antiquity*, New York.

Watts, C. (1987) 'A pattern language for houses at Pompeii, Herculaneum and Ostia', Ph.D. thesis, University of Texas at Austin.

Weber, M. (1958) *The City*, New York.

Whittaker, C.R. (1990) 'The consumer city revisited: the *vicus* and the city', *Journal of Roman Archaeology* 3: 110–18.

Williams, R. (1973) *The Countryside and the City*, Oxford.

Williams-Thorpe, O. (1988) 'Provenancing and archaeology of Roman millstones from the Mediterranean area', *Journal of Archaeological Science* 15: 253–305.

Wilson, E. (1991) *The Sphinx in the City*, London.

Wiseman, T.P. (1977) 'Cicero *pro Sulla* 60–61', *Liverpool Classical Monthly* 2: 21–2.

Wolff, J. (1992) 'The real city, discursive city, the disappearing city: postmodernism and urban sociology', *Theory and Society* 24(4): 553–60.

Zanker, P. (1988a) *Pompeji: Stadtbilder als Spiegel von Gesellschaft und Herrschaftsform*, Mainz.

—— (1988b) *The Power of Images in the Age of Augustus*, Ann Arbor.

INDEX